Warren Hunt

# TODAY'S STORY OF
# JESUS

# TODAY'S STORY OF
# JESUS

Abridged by David L. Edwards
from
Good News Bible in Today's English Version

Illustrated by Guido Bertello

COLLINS WORLD
Cleveland, Ohio 44111

First published in this edition 1976
Published by Collins + World Publishers, Cleveland, Ohio
© Text 1966, 1971, 1976 American Bible Society, New York
© Illustrations 1976 William Collins Sons and Company Limited
Text printed in the United States
Illustrations printed in Great Britain

Library of Congress Cataloging in Publication Data
Edwards, David Lawrence.
Today's story of Jesus.
1. Jesus Christ — Biography — Sources, Biblica.
2. Christian biography — Palestine.
I. Bertello. II. Bible. N. T. English. Today's English. III. Title.
BT299.2.E35  1976   232.9'01   76-42223   ISBN 0-529-05331-4

# Preface

This book tells the story of Jesus in the words of the Bible. It contains most of what is given to us in the gospels of Mark, Luke and Matthew, together with extracts from John's gospel, the Acts of the Apostles, and the letters.

There are four gospels because the New Testament grew out of the meetings of the early Christians. A letter might be read from Paul or another leader of the Church, and a teacher would, as he talked, repeat some of the things that Jesus said or did. These things were then written down and arranged in order. It was like stringing beads together to make a necklace. But four gospels were put together, because four different congregations preferred the arrangement made by four different evangelists.

What I have done in this book is to make one story. It is like gathering the best beads on one string. I have collected whole paragraphs, printing each of these as it stands in one of the gospels and only occasionally adding, or cutting out, a few words so that one paragraph may easily connect with the next one. I have added a very brief summary at the beginning of each chapter.

I hope that this arrangement will help readers to understand and love this story in its simplicity and power. After this fresh telling of the greatest story in the world, the extracts from the rest of the New Testament will, I pray, help readers to understand how the early Christians responded — and how we today can and should respond. For part of the story of Jesus is the story of how millions of followers have been fascinated and liberated by him.

The translation used is *Today's English Version,* which is a distinctly new translation of the original Greek. The basic draft of this translation was prepared by Dr. Robert G. Bratcher. It was submitted to a panel of specialists for study and finally reviewed and approved by the Translations Committee of the American Bible Society.

My book on *Jesus for Modern Man* (1975) discusses some of the historical problems.

DAVID L. EDWARDS

# Contents

# 1
# When Jesus was Young

*Jesus was a poor boy. When he was young, people did not see how great he would be. But many years later Luke and Matthew told the stories which we remember every Christmas, and which give the message that Mary's son was really Christ the Lord, the "Messiah" (born to be King of the Jews).*

*Only one story is told by Luke about Jesus as a boy: the story of his visit to the temple in Jerusalem. It shows that already Jesus knew God as his Father. To him, the temple was his Father's house.*

*There is another story told in these parts of the Bible, about a boy called John, the son of Zechariah and Elizabeth. This was John the Baptist, and about him it was said:*

*"You will go ahead of the Lord*
*to prepare his way for him."*

## The First Christmas

*The Birth of Jesus Announced*

God sent the angel Gabriel to a town in Galilee named Nazareth. He had a message for a girl promised in marriage to a man named Joseph, who was a descendant of King David. The girl's name was Mary. The angel came to her and said, "Peace be with you! The Lord is with you and has greatly blessed you!"

Mary was deeply troubled by the angel's message, and she wondered what his words meant. The angel said to her, "Don't be afraid, Mary, because God has been gracious to you. You will become pregnant and give birth to a son, and you will name him Jesus. He will be great and will be called the Son of the Most High God. The Lord God will make him a king, as his ancestor David was, and he will be the king of the descendants of Jacob forever; his kingdom will never end!"

Mary said to the angel, "I am a virgin. How, then, can this be?"

The angel answered, "The Holy Spirit will come on you, and God's power will rest upon you. For this reason the holy child will be called the Son of God. Remember your relative Elizabeth. It is said that she cannot have children; but she herself is now six months pregnant, even though she is very old. For there is nothing that God cannot do."

"I am the Lord's servant," said Mary; "may it happen to me as you have said." And the angel left her.

*Mary Visits Elizabeth*

Soon afterwards Mary got ready and hurried off to a town in the hill country of Judea. She went into Zechariah's house and greeted Elizabeth. When Elizabeth heard Mary's greeting, the baby moved within her. Elizabeth was filled with the Holy Spirit, and spoke in a loud voice, "You are the most blessed of all women, and blessed is the child you will bear! Why should this great thing happen to me, that my Lord's mother comes to visit me? For as soon as I heard your greeting, the baby within jumped with gladness. How happy are you to believe that the Lord's message to you will come true!"

*Mary's Song of Praise*

Mary said,
"My heart praises the Lord;
my soul is glad because of God my Savior,
for he has remembered me, his lowly servant!
From now on all people will call me happy, because of the great
things the Mighty God has done for me.
His name is holy;
From one generation to another he shows mercy to those who fear
him.
He has stretched out his mighty arm
and scattered the proud with all their plans.
He has brought down mighty kings from their thrones,
and lifted up the lowly.
He has filled the hungry with good things, and sent the rich away
with empty hands.
He has kept the promise he made to our ancestors,
and has come to the help of his servant Israel,
He has remembered to show mercy to Abraham
and to all his descendants forever!"

Mary stayed about three months with Elizabeth and then went back
home.

*The Birth of Jesus*

At that time Emperor Augustus ordered a census to be taken throughout
the Roman Empire. When this first census took place, Quirinius was the
governor of Syria. Everyone, then, went to register himself, each to his
own home town.

Joseph went from the town of Nazareth in Galilee to the town of
Bethlehem in Judea, the birthplace of King David. Joseph went there
because he was a descendant of David. He went to register with Mary,
who was promised in marriage to him. She was pregnant, and while they
were in Bethlehem, the time came for her to have her baby. She gave
birth to her first son, wrapped him in cloths and laid him in a manger —
there was no room for them to stay in the inn.

*The Shepherds and the Angels*

There were some shepherds in that part of the country who were
spending the night in the fields, taking care of their flocks. An angel of
the Lord appeared to them, and the glory of the Lord shone over them.
They were terribly afraid, but the angel said to them, "Don't be
afraid! I am here with good news for you, which will bring great joy to
all the people. This very day in David's town your Savior was born —

Christ the Lord! And this is what will prove it to you: you will find a baby wrapped in cloths and lying in a manger."

Suddenly a great army of heaven's angels appeared with the angel, singing praises to God:

"Glory to God in the highest heaven,
and peace on earth to those with whom he is pleased!"

When the angels went away from them back into heaven, the shepherds said to one another, "Let's go to Bethlehem and see this thing that has happened, which the Lord has told us."

So they hurried off and found Mary and Joseph and saw the baby lying in the manger. When the shepherds saw him they told them what the angel had said about the child. All who heard it were amazed at what the shepherds said. Mary remembered all these things and thought deeply about them. The shepherds went back, singing praises to God for all they had heard and seen; it had been just as the angel had told them.

*Jesus is Named*

A week later, when the time came for the baby to be circumcised, he was named Jesus, the name which the angel had given him before he had been conceived.

## Jesus is Presented in the Temple

The time came for Joseph and Mary to perform the ceremony of purification as the Law of Moses commanded. So they took the child to Jerusalem to present him to the Lord, as it is written in the law of the Lord, "Every first-born male is to be dedicated to the Lord." They also went to offer a sacrifice of a pair of doves or two young pigeons, as required by the law of the Lord.

At that time there was a man living in Jerusalem named Simeon. He was a good, God-fearing man and was waiting for Israel to be saved. The Holy Spirit was with him and had assured him that he would not die before he had seen the Lord's promised Messiah. Led by the Spirit, Simeon went into the Temple. When the parents brought the child Jesus into the Temple to do for him what the Law required, Simeon took the child in his arms, and gave thanks to God:

"Now, Lord, you have kept your promise,
and you may let your servant go in peace.
With my own eyes I have seen your salvation,
which you have prepared in the presence of all peoples:
A light to reveal your will to the Gentiles, and bring glory to your
people Israel."

The child's father and mother were amazed at the things Simeon said about him. Simeon blessed them and said to Mary, his mother, "This child is chosen by God for the destruction and the salvation of many in Israel. He will be a sign from God which many people will speak against, and so reveal their secret thoughts. And sorrow, like a sharp sword, will break your own heart."

There was a very old prophetess a widow named Anna, daughter of Phanuel of the tribe of Asher. She had been married for only seven years, and was now eighty-four years old. She never left the Temple; day and night she worshiped God, fasting and praying. That very same hour she arrived and gave thanks to God and spoke about the child to all who were waiting for God to set Jerusalem free.

## The Wise Men in Matthew's Gospel

*Visitors from the East*

Jesus was born in the town of Bethlehem, in Judea, during the time when Herod was king. Soon afterward, some men who studied the stars came from the East to Jerusalem and asked, "Where is the baby born to be the king of the Jews? We saw his star when it came up in the east, and we have come to worship him."

When King Herod heard about this he was very upset, and so was everyone else in Jerusalem. He called together all the chief priests and the teachers of the Law and asked them, "Where will the Messiah be born."

"In the town of Bethlehem, in Judea," they answered. "For this is what the prophet wrote,

'Bethlehem, in the land of Judah,
    you are by no means the least of the leading cities of Judah;
for from you will come a leader who will guide my people Israel.'"

So Herod called the visitors from the East to a secret meeting and found out from them the exact time the star had appeared. Then he sent them to Bethlehem with these instructions: "Go and make a careful search for the child: and when you find him let me know, so that I may go and worship him."

And so they left, and on their way they saw the same star they had seen in the East. When they saw it, how happy they were, what joy was theirs. It went ahead of them until it stopped over the place where the child was. They went into the house and when they saw the child with his mother Mary they knelt down and worshiped him: They brought out their gifts of gold, frankincense, and myrrh, and presented them to him.

Then they returned to their country by another road, since God had warned them in a dream not to go back to Herod.

### The Escape to Egypt

After they had left, an angel of the Lord appeared in a dream to Joseph and said, Herod will be looking for the child in order to kill him. So get up, take the child and his mother and escape to Egypt, and stay there until I tell you to leave.

Joseph got up, took the child and his mother, and left during the night for Egypt, where he stayed until Herod died.

### The Killing of the Children

When Herod realized that the visitors from the East had tricked him, he was furious. He gave orders to kill all the boys in Bethlehem and its neighborhood who were two years old and younger — this was done in accordance with what he had learned from the visitors about the time when the star had appeared.

### The Return from Egypt

After Herod had died, an angel of the Lord appeared in a dream to Joseph in Egypt and said, "Get up, take the child and his mother, and

go back to the land of Israel, because those who tried to kill the child are dead." So Joseph got up, took the child and his mother, and went back to Israel.

But when Joseph heard that Archelaus had succeeded his father Herod as king of Judea, he was afraid to go there. He was given more instructions in a dream, so he went to the province of Galilee and made his home in a town name Nazareth.

**The Boy Jesus in the Temple**

Every year the parents of Jesus went to Jerusalem for the Passover Festival. When Jesus was twelve years old, they went to the festival as usual.

18

When the festival was over, they started back home, but the boy Jesus stayed in Jerusalem. His parents did not know this; they thought that he was with the group, so they traveled a whole day, and then started looking for him among their relatives and friends. They did not find him, so they went back to Jerusalem looking for him. On the third day they found him in the Temple, sitting with the Jewish teachers, listening to them and asking questions. All who heard him were amazed at his intelligent answers. His parents were astonished when they saw him, and his mother said to him, "Son, why have you done this to us? Your father and I have been terribly worried trying to find you."

He answered them, "Why did you have to look for me? Didn't you know that I had to be in my Father's house?"

So Jesus went back with them to Nazareth, where he was obedient to them. His mother treasured all these things in her heart. And Jesus grew, both in body and in wisdom, gaining favor with God and men.

## John the Baptist, God's Messenger

*The Birth of John the Baptist*

The time came for Elizabeth to have her baby, and she gave birth to a son. Her neighbors and relatives heard how wonderfully good the Lord had been to her, and they all rejoiced with her.

When the baby was a week old, they came to circumcise him and they were going to name him Zechariah, after his father. But his mother said, "No! His name will be John."

*Zechariah's Prophecy*

John's father Zechariah was filled with the Holy Spirit, and he spoke God's message,

"Let us praise the Lord, the God of Israel!
    He has come to the help of his people and has set them free.
He has provided for us a mighty Savior,
    a descendant of his servant David.
He promised through his holy prophets long ago
    that he would save us from our enemies,
    from the power of all those who hate us.
He said he would show mercy to our ancestors
    and remember his sacred covenant.
With a solemn promise to our ancestor Abraham,
    he promised to rescue us from our enemies
    and allow us to serve him without fear,
    so that we might be holy and righteous before him,
    all the days of our life.

"You, my child, will be called a prophet of the Most High God.
You will go ahead of the Lord to prepare his road for him;
    to tell his people that they will be saved by having their sins
    forgiven.
Our God is merciful and tender.
He will cause the bright dawn of salvation to rise on us
    and to shine from heaven on all those who live in the dark
    shadow of death,
    to guide our steps into the path of peace."

The child grew and developed in body and spirit. He lived in the desert until the day when he appeared publicly to the people of Israel.

It was the fifteenth year of the rule of Emperor Tiberius; Pontius Pilate was governor of Judea, Herod was ruler of Galilee, and his brother Philip was ruler of the territory of Iturea and Trachonitis; Lysanias was ruler of Abilene, and Annas and Caiaphas were high priests. At that time the word of God came to John son of Zechariah in the desert. So John went throughout the whole territory of the Jordan River, preaching, "Turn away from your sins and be baptized, and God will forgive your sins," As it is written in the book of the prophet Isaiah:

> "Someone is shouting in the desert:
>    'Get the road ready for the Lord;
>    make a straight path for him to travel!
> Every valley must be filled up,
>    every hill and mountain leveled off.
> The winding roads must be made straight,
>    and the rough paths made smooth.
> All mankind will see God's salvation!' "

Crowds of people came out to John to be baptized by him. "You snakes!" he said to them. "Who told you that you could escape from the punishment God is about to send? Do those things that will show that you have turned from your sins. And don't start saying among yourselves that Abraham is our ancestor. I tell you that God can take these rocks and make descendants for Abraham! The ax is ready to cut down the trees at the roots; every tree that does not bear good fruit will be cut down and thrown in the fire."

The people asked him. "What are we to do, then?"

He answered, "Whoever has two shirts must give one to the man who has none, and whoever has food must share it."

Some tax collectors came to be baptized, and they asked him, "Teacher, what are we to do?"

"Don't collect more than is legal," he told them.

Some soldiers also asked him, "What about us? What are we to do?"

He said to them, "Don't take money from anyone by force or accuse anyone falsely. Be content with your pay."

People's hopes began to rise, and they began to wonder whether John perhaps might be the Messiah. So John said to all of them, "I baptize you with water, but someone is coming who is much greater than I am. I am not good enough even to untie his sandals. He will baptize you with the Holy Spirit and fire. He has his winnowing shovel with him, to thresh out all the grain and gather the wheat into his barn; but he will burn the chaff in a fire that never goes out."

In many different ways John preached the Good News to the people and urged them to change their ways.

# 2
# How Jesus Lived

*After he had been baptized by John in the river Jordan, Jesus turned to what it was God wanted him to do. He was tempted to take wrong ways, but finally he depended humbly on God. So he began his work for God, healing many people.*

*In those days everyone thought that diseases were caused by demons, or evil spirits, who lived inside the sick person. So when people saw Jesus healing minds and bodies by the power of his love and faith, they said: "This man is able to give orders to the evil spirits!" But Jesus not only cured diseases. He also set people free from their sins — from everything that separated them from true life and true joy. People said, "We have never seen anything like this!" And some of them, specially the twelve apostles, gave up everything in order to follow him when he called them. Jesus said, "Whoever does what God wants him to do is my brother, my sister, my mother."*

*Jesus spread the good news of God's reign giving people peace and health. He gave them courage by being with them. Strange stories are told about his powers; he stopped a storm, fed thousands and walked on water. The whole life of Jesus showed a strange power. Jesus himself claimed that it was the power of God in action. The strange things which Jesus did were not intended to draw attention to him. They were intended to show that God's Kingdom was a kingdom of peace and health.*

## Jesus is Baptized and Tempted

### The Baptism of Jesus

At that time Jesus arrived from Galilee at the Jordan and came to John to be baptized by him. But John tried to make him change his mind. "I ought to be baptized by you," John said, "and yet you come to me!"

But Jesus answered him, "Let it be so for now. For in this way we shall do all that God requires." So John agreed.

As soon as Jesus was baptized, he came up out of the water. Then heaven was opened to him, and he saw the Spirit of God coming down like a dove and lighting on him. Then a voice said from heaven, "This is my own dear Son, with whom I am pleased."

*The Temptation of Jesus*

Then the Spirit led Jesus into the desert to be tempted by the Devil. After spending forty days and nights without food, Jesus was hungry. Then the Devil came to him and said, "If you are God's Son, order these stones to turn into bread."

Jesus answered, "The scripture says, 'Man cannot live on bread alone, but needs every word that God speaks.'"

Then the Devil took Jesus to Jerusalem, the Holy City, set him on the highest point of the Temple, and said to him, "If you are God's Son, throw yourself down, for the scripture says,

'God will give orders to his angels about you;
    they will hold you up with their hands,
    so that not even your feet will be hurt on the stones.'"

Jesus answered, "But the scripture also says, 'Do not put the Lord your God to the test.'"

Then the Devil took Jesus to a very high mountain and showed him all the kingdoms of the world in all their greatness. "All this I will give you," the Devil said, "if you kneel down and worship me."

Then Jesus answered, "Go away, Satan! The scripture says, 'Worship the Lord your God and serve only him!'"

Then the Devil left Jesus; and angels came and helped Jesus.

## Jesus Begins his Work

*Jesus Calls Four Fishermen*

After John had been put in prison, Jesus went to Galilee and preached the Good News from God. "The right time has come," he said, "and the Kingdom of God is near! Turn away from your sins and believe the Good News!"

As Jesus walked along the shore of Lake Galilee, he saw two fishermen, Simon and his brother Andrew, catching fish with a net. Jesus said to them, "Come with me and I will teach you to catch men." At once they left their nets and went with him.

He went a little farther on and saw two other brothers, James and John, the sons of Zebedee. They were in their boat getting their nets ready. As soon as Jesus saw them, he called them; they left their father Zebedee in the boat with the hired men and went with Jesus.

*A Man with an Evil Spirit*

Jesus and his disciples came to the town of Capernaum, and on the next Sabbath Jesus went to the synagogue and began to teach. The people who heard him were amazed at the way he taught, for he wasn't like the teachers of the Law; instead, he taught with authority.

*Opposite: the baptism of Jesus (text on page 23)*

Just then a man with an evil spirit came into the synagogue and screamed, "What do you want with us, Jesus of Nazareth? Are you here to destroy us? I know who you are — you are God's holy messenger!"

Jesus ordered the spirit, "Be quiet, and come out of the man!"

The evil spirit shook the man hard, gave a loud scream, and came out of him. The people were all so amazed that they started saying to one another, "What is this? Is it some kind of new teaching? This man has authority to give orders to the evil spirits, and they obey him!"

And so the news about Jesus spread quickly everywhere in the province of Galilee.

*Jesus Heals Many People*

Jesus and his disciples, including James and John, left the synagogue and went straight to the home of Simon and Andrew. Simon's mother-in-law was sick in bed with a fever, and as soon as Jesus arrived he was told about her. He went to her, took her by the hand and helped her up. The fever left her and she began to wait on them.

After the sun had set and evening had come, people brought to Jesus all the sick and those who had demons. All the people of the town gathered in front of the house. Jesus healed many who were sick with all kinds of diseases and drove out many demons. He would not let the demons say anything, because they knew who he was.

*Jesus Preaches in Galilee*

Very early the next morning, long before daylight, Jesus got up and left the house. He went out of town to a lonely place, where he prayed. But Simon and his companions went out searching for him, and when they found him they said, "Everyone is looking for you."

But Jesus answered, "We must go on to the other villages round here. I have to preach in them also, because that is why I came."

So he traveled all over Galilee, preaching in the synagogues and driving out demons.

*Jesus Heals a Man*

A man suffering from a dreaded skin disease came to Jesus, knelt down, and begged him for help. "If you want to," he said, "you can make me clean."

Jesus was filled with pity, and reached out and touched him. "I do want to," he answered. "Be clean!" At once the disease left the man and he was clean. Then Jesus spoke sternly to him and sent him away at once, after saying to him, "Listen, don't tell anyone about this. But go straight to the priest and let him examine you; then in order to prove to everyone that you are cured, offer the sacrifice that Moses ordered."

*Opposite: Jesus calls the fishermen (text on page 25)*

But the man went away and began to spread the news everywhere. Indeed, he talked so much that Jesus could not go into a town publicly. Instead, he stayed out in lonely places, and people came to him from everywhere.

### Jesus Heals a Paralyzed Man

A few days later Jesus went back to Capernaum, and the news spread that he was at home. So many people came together that there was no room left, not even out in front of the door. Jesus was preaching the message to them, when four men arrived carrying a paralyzed man to Jesus. Because of the crowd, however, they could not get the man to him. So they made a hole in the roof right above the place where Jesus was. When they had made an opening, they let the man down, lying on his mat. Seeing how much faith they had, Jesus said to the paralyzed man, "My son, your sins are forgiven."

Some teachers of the Law who were sitting there thought to themselves, "How does he dare talk like this? This is blasphemy! God is the only one who can forgive sins!"

At once Jesus knew what they were thinking, so he said to them, "Why do you think such things? Is it easier to say to this paralyzed man, 'Your sins are forgiven,' or to say, 'Get up, pick up your mat, and walk'? I will prove to you, then, that the Son of Man has authority on earth to forgive sins." So he said to the paralyzed man, "I tell you, get up, pick up your mat, and go home!"

While they all watched, the man got up, picked up his mat and hurried away. They were all completely amazed and praised God, saying, "We have never seen anything like this!"

### Jesus Calls Matthew

Jesus left that place, and as he walked along he saw a tax collector, named Matthew, sitting in his office. He said to him, "Follow me."

Matthew got up and followed him.

While Jesus was having a meal in Matthew's house, many tax collectors and other outcasts came and joined Jesus and his disciples at the table. Some Pharisees saw this and said to his disciples, "Why does your teacher eat with such people?"

Jesus heard them and answered, "People who are well do not need a doctor, but only those who are sick. Go and find out what is meant by the scripture that says, 'It is kindness that I want, not animal sacrifices.' I have not come to call the respectable people, but outcasts."

## The Question about Fasting

On one occasion the followers of John the Baptist and the Pharisees were fasting. Some people came to Jesus and asked him. "Why is it that the disciples of John the Baptist and the disciples of the Pharisees fast, but yours do not?"

Jesus answered, "Do you expect the guests at a wedding party to go without food? Of course not! As long as the bridegroom is with them they will not do that. But the day will come when the bridegroom will be taken away from them, and then they will fast.

"No one uses a piece of new cloth to patch up an old coat, because the new patch will shrink and tear off some of the old cloth, making an even bigger hole. Nor does anyone pour new wine into used wineskins, because the wine will burst the skins, and both the wine and the skins will be ruined. Instead, new wine must be poured into fresh wineskins."

## Jesus Has Pity for the People

Jesus went round visiting all the towns and villages. He taught in their synagogues, preached the Good News about the Kingdom, and healed people with every kind of disease and sickness. As he saw the crowds, his heart was filled with pity for them, because they were worried and helpless, like sheep without a shepherd. So he said to his disciples, "The harvest is large, but there are few workers to gather it in. Pray to the owner of the harvest that he will send out workers to gather in his harvest."

# The New Family Chosen By Jesus

## A Crowd by the Lake

Jesus and his disciples went away to Lake Galilee, and a large crowd followed him. They had come from Galilee, from Judea, from Jerusalem, from the territory of Idumea, from the territory on the east side of the Jordan, and from the region around the cities of Tyre and Sidon. All these people came to Jesus because they had heard of the things he was doing. The crowd was so large that Jesus told his disciples to get a boat ready for him, so that the people would not crush him. He had healed many people, and all the sick kept pushing their way to him in order to touch him. And whenever the people who had evil spirits in them saw him they would fall down before him and scream. "You are the Son of God!"

Jesus sternly ordered the evil spirits not to tell anyone who he was.

30

## Jesus Chooses the Twelve Apostles

Then Jesus went up a hill and called to himself the men he wanted. They came to him, and he chose twelve, whom he named apostles. "I have chosen you to be with me," he told them: "I will also send you out to preach, and you will have authority to drive out demons."

These are the twelve he chose: Simon (Jesus gave him the name Peter); James and his brother John, the sons of Zebedee (Jesus gave them the name Boanerges, which means "Men of Thunder"); Andrew, Philip, Bartholomew, Matthew, Thomas, James the son of Alphaeus, Thaddaeus, Simon the Patriot, and Judas Iscariot, who betrayed Jesus.

## Jesus' Mother and Brothers

Then Jesus went home. Again such a large crowd gathered that Jesus and his disciples had no time to eat. When his family heard about it, they set out to take charge of him, because people were saying, "He's gone mad!" Then Jesus' mother and brothers arrived. They stood outside the house and sent in a message, asking for him. A crowd was sitting round Jesus, and they said to him, "Look, your mother and your brothers and sisters are outside, and they want you."

Jesus answered, "Who is my mother? Who are my brothers?" He looked at the people sitting round him and said, "Look! Here are my mother and my brothers! Whoever does what God wants him to do is my brother, my sister, my mother."

## Jesus Rejected at Nazareth

Then Jesus went to Nazareth, where he had been brought up, and on the Sabbath day he went as usual to the synagogue. He stood up to read the Scriptures, and was handed the book of the prophet Isaiah. He unrolled the scroll and found the place where it is written.

"The Spirit of the Lord is upon me,
    because he has chosen me to bring good news to the poor.
He has sent me to proclaim liberty to the captives
    and recovery of sight to the blind,
to set free the oppressed,
    and announce that the time has come when the Lord will save
    his people."

Jesus rolled up the scroll, gave it back to the attendant, and sat down. All the people in the synagogue had their eyes fixed on him, as he said to them, "This passage of scripture has come true today, as you heard it being read."

They were all well impressed with him, and marveled at the eloquent words that he spoke. They said, "Isn't he the son of Joseph?"

He said to them, "I am sure that you will quote this proverb to me,

'Doctor, heal yourself.' You will also tell me to do here in my home town the same things you heard were done in Capernaum.' I tell you this," Jesus added, "a prophet is never welcomed in his home town. Listen to me: it is true that there were many widows in Israel during the time of Elijah, when there was no rain for three and a half years and a severe famine spread throughout the whole land. Yet Elijah was not sent to anyone in Israel, but only to a widow living in Zarephath in the territory of Sidon. And there were many people suffering from a dreaded skin disease who lived in Israel during the time of the prophet Elisha; yet not one of them was healed, but only Naaman the Syrian."

When the people in the synagogue heard this, they were filled with anger. They rose up, dragged Jesus out of town, and took him to the top of the hill on which their town was built. They meant to throw him over the cliff, but he walked through the middle of the crowd and went his way.

## The Good News is Spread by Word and Deed

*Jesus Heals a Roman Officer's Servant*

Jesus went to Capernaum. A Roman officer there had a servant who was very dear to him; the man was sick and about to die. When the officer heard about Jesus, he sent some Jewish elders to ask him to come and heal his servant. They came to Jesus and begged him earnestly, "This man really deserves your help. He loves our people and he himself built a synagogue for us."

So Jesus went with them. He was not far from the house when the officer sent friends to tell him, "Sir, don't trouble yourself. I do not deserve to have you come into my house, neither do I consider myself worthy to come to you in person. Just give the order and my servant will get well. I, too, am a man placed under the authority of superior officers, and I have soldiers under me. I order this one, 'Go!' and he goes; I order that one, 'Come!' and he comes; and I order my slave, 'Do this!' and he does it."

Jesus was surprised when he heard this; he turned round and said to the crowd following him, "I tell you, I have never found faith like this, not even in Israel!"

The messengers went back to the officer's house and found his servant well.

*Jesus Raises a Widow's Son*

Soon afterward Jesus went to a town named Nain, accompanied by his disciples and a large crowd. Just as he arrived at the gate of the town, a funeral procession was coming out. The dead man was the only son of a

woman who was a widow, and a large crowd from the town was with her. When the Lord saw her, his heart was filled with pity for her, and he said to her, "Don't cry." Then he walked over and touched the coffin, and the men carrying it stopped. Jesus said, "Young man! Get up, I tell you!" The dead man sat up and began to talk, and Jesus gave him back to his mother.

They all were filled with fear, and praised God. "A great prophet has appeared among us!" they said, "God has come to save his people!"


*The Messengers from John the Baptist*

When John's disciples told him about all these things, he called two of them and sent them to the Lord to ask him, "Are you the one John said was going to come, or should we expect someone else?"

When they came to Jesus, they said, "John the Baptist sent us to ask if you are the one he said was going to come, or should we expect someone else?'"

At that very time Jesus healed many people from their sicknesses, diseases, and evil spirits, and gave sight to many blind people. He answered John's messengers, "Go back and tell John what you have seen and heard: the blind can see, the lame can walk, those who suffer from dreaded skin diseases are made clean, the deaf can hear, the dead are raised to life, and the Good News is preached to the poor. How happy is he who has no doubts about me!"

After John's messengers had left, Jesus began to speak about him to the crowds: "When you went out to John in the desert, what did you expect to see? A blade of grass bending in the wind? What did you go out to see? A man dressed up in fancy clothes? People who dress like that and live in luxury are found in palaces! Tell me, what did you go out to see? A prophet? Yes indeed, but you saw much more than a prophet. For John is the one of whom the scripture says: 'God said, I will send my messenger ahead of you to open the way for you.' I tell you," Jesus added, "John is greater than any man who has ever lived. But he who is least in the Kingdom of God is greater than John."

Jesus continued, "Now, to what can I compare the people of this day? What are they like? They are like children sitting in the market place. One group shouts to the other, 'We played wedding music for you, but you wouldn't dance! We sang funeral songs, but you wouldn't cry!' John the Baptist came, and he fasted and drank no wine, and you said, 'He has a demon in him!' The Son of Man came, and he ate and drank, and you said, 'Look at this man! He is a glutton and wine-drinker, a friend of tax collectors and other outcasts!' God's wisdom, however, is shown to be true by all who accept it."

## Jesus at the Home of Simon the Pharisee

A Pharisee invited Jesus to have dinner with him, and Jesus went to his house and sat down to eat. In that town was a woman who lived a sinful life. She heard that Jesus was eating in the Pharisee's house, so she brought an alabaster jar full of perfume and stood behind Jesus, by his feet, crying and wetting his feet with her tears. Then she dried his feet with her hair, kissed them, and poured the perfume on them. When the Pharisee saw this, he said to himself, "If this man really were a prophet, he would know who this woman is who is touching him; he would know what kind of sinful life she lives!"

Jesus spoke up and said to him. "Simon, I have something to tell you."

"Yes, Teacher," he said, "tell me."

"There were two men who owed money to a moneylender," Jesus began: "One owed him five hundred silver coins and the other one fifty silver coins. Neither one could pay him back, so he canceled the debts of both. Which one, then, will love him more?"

"I suppose," answered Simon, "that it would be the one who was forgiven more."

"You are right," said Jesus. Then he turned to the woman and said to Simon, "Do you see this woman? I came into your home, and you gave me no water for my feet, but she has washed my feet with her tears and dried them with her hair. You did not welcome me with a kiss, but she has not stopped kissing my feet since I came. You provided no olive oil for my head, but she has covered my feet with perfume. I tell you, then, the great love she has shown proves that her many sins have been forgiven. But whoever has been forgiven little shows only a little love."

Then Jesus said to the woman, "Your sins are forgiven."

The others sitting at the table began to say to themselves, "Who is this, who even forgives sins?"

But Jesus said to the woman, "Your faith has saved you; go in peace."

## Women who Accompanied Jesus

Some time later Jesus traveled through towns and villages, preaching the Good News about the Kingdom of God. The twelve disciples went with him, and so did some women who had been healed of evil spirits and diseases: Mary (who was called Magdalene), from whom seven demons had been driven out; Joanna, whose husband Chuza was an officer in Herod's court; and Suzanna, and many other women who used their own resources to help Jesus and his disciples.

## Jesus Heals a Boy with an Evil Spirit

Some teachers of the Law were arguing with the disciples. When the

people saw Jesus, they were greatly surprised and ran to him and greeted him. Jesus asked his disciples, "What are you arguing with them about?"

A man in the crowd answered, "Teacher, I brought my son to you, because he has an evil spirit in him and cannot talk. Whenever the spirit attacks him, it throws him to the ground, and he foams at the mouth, grits his teeth, and becomes stiff all over. I asked your disciples to drive the spirit out, but they could not."

Jesus said to them, "How unbelieving you people are! How long must I stay with you? How long do I have to put up with you? Bring the boy to me!" They brought him to Jesus.

As soon as the spirit saw Jesus, it threw the boy into a fit, so that he fell on the ground and rolled around, foaming at the mouth. "How long has he been like this?" Jesus asked the father.

"Ever since he was a child," he replied. "Many times the evil spirit has tried to kill him by throwing him in the fire and into water. Have pity on us and help us, if you possibly can!"

"Yes," said Jesus, "if you yourself can! Everything is possible for the person who has faith."

The father at once cried out, "I do have faith, but not enough. Help me have more!"

Jesus noticed that the crowd was closing in on them, so he gave a command to the evil spirit. "Deaf and dumb spirit," he said, "I order you to come out of the boy and never go into him again!"

The spirit screamed, threw the boy into a bad fit, and came out. The boy looked like a corpse, and everyone said, "He is dead!" But Jesus took the boy by the hand and helped him rise, and he stood up.

After Jesus had gone indoors, his disciples asked him privately, "Why couldn't we drive the spirit out?"

"Only prayer can drive this kind out," answered Jesus; "nothing else can."

### Jesus Calms a Storm

One evening Jesus said to his disciples, "Let us go across to the other side of the lake." So they left the crowd; the disciples got into the boat in which Jesus was already sitting, and they took him with them. Other boats were there too. A very strong wind blew up and the waves began to spill over into the boat, so that it was about to fill with water. Jesus was in the back of the boat, sleeping with his head on a pillow. The disciples woke him up and said, "Teacher, don't you care that we are about to die?"

Jesus stood up and commanded the wind, "Be quiet!" and he said to the waves, "Be still!" The wind died down, and there was a great calm.

Then Jesus said to his disciples, "Why are you frightened? Do you still have no faith?"

But they were terribly afraid and began to say to one another, "Who is this man? Even the wind and the waves obey him!"

*Jesus Heals a Man with Evil Spirits*

Jesus and his disciples arrived on the other side of Lake Galilee, in the territory of Gerasa. As soon as Jesus got out of the boat he was met by a man who came out of the burial caves there. This man had an evil spirit in him and lived among the tombs. Nobody could keep him tied with chains any more; many times his feet and hands had been tied, but every time he broke the chains and smashed the irons on his feet. He was too strong for anyone to control him. Day and night he wandered among the tombs and through the hills, screaming and cutting himself with stones.

He was some distance away when he saw Jesus; so he ran, fell on his knees before him, and screamed in a loud voice, "Jesus, Son of the Most High God! What do you want with me? For God's sake, I beg you, don't punish me!" (He said this because Jesus was saying, "Evil spirit, come out of this man!")

So Jesus asked him, "What is your name?"

The man answered, "My name is 'Mob' — there are so many of us!" And he kept begging Jesus not to send the evil spirits out of that region.

There was a large herd of pigs near by, feeding on a hillside. So the spirits begged Jesus, "Send us to the pigs, and let us go into them." He let them go, and the evil spirits went out of the man and entered the pigs. The whole herd — about two thousand pigs in all — rushed down the side of the cliff into the lake and was drowned.

The men who had been taking care of the pigs ran away and spread the news in the town and among the farms. People went out to see what had happened, and when they came to Jesus, they saw the man who used to have the mob of demons in him. He was sitting there, clothed and in his right mind; and they were all afraid. Those who had seen it told the people what had happened to the man with the demons, and about the pigs. So they began to ask Jesus to leave their territory.

As Jesus was getting into the boat, the man who had had the demons begged him, "Let me go with you!"

But Jesus would not let him. Instead, he told him, "Go back home to your family and tell them how much the Lord has done for you, and how kind he has been to you."

So the man left and went all through the Ten Towns, telling what Jesus had done for him; and all who heard it were amazed.

Jesus went back across to the other side of the lake. There at the lakeside a large crowd gathered round him. Jairus, an official of the local synagogue, arrived, and when he saw Jesus, he threw himself down at his feet and begged him earnestly, "My little daughter is very sick. Please come and place your hands on her, so that she will get well and live!"

Then Jesus started off with him. So many people were going along with Jesus that they were crowding him from every side.

There was a woman who had suffered terribly from severe bleeding for twelve years, even though she had been treated by many doctors. She had spent all her money, but instead of getting better she got worse all the time. She had heard about Jesus, so she came in the crowd behind him, saying to herself, "If I just touch his clothes, I will get well."

She touched his cloak and her bleeding stopped at once; and she had the feeling inside herself that she was healed of her trouble. At once Jesus knew that power had gone out of him, so he turned round in the crowd and asked, "Who touched my clothes?"

His disciples answered, "You see how the people are crowding you; why do you ask who touched you?"

But Jesus kept looking round to see who had done it. The woman realized what had happened to her, so she came, trembling with fear, knelt at his feet, and told him the whole truth. Jesus said to her, "My daughter, your faith has made you well. Go in peace, and be healed of your trouble."

While Jesus was saying this, some messengers came from Jairus' house and told him, "Your daughter has died. Why bother the teacher any longer?"

Jesus paid no attention to what they said, but told him, "Don't be afraid, only believe." Then he did not let anyone else go on with him except Peter and James and his brother John. They arrived at Jairus' house, where Jesus saw the confusion and heard all the loud crying and wailing. He went in and said to them, "Why all this confusion? Why are you crying? The child is not dead — she is only sleeping!"

They started making fun of him, so he put them all out, took the child's father and mother, and his three disciples, and went into the room where the child was lying. He took her by the hand and said to her, *"Talitha, koum,"* which means, "Little girl! I tell you to get up!"

She got up at once and started walking around. (She was twelve years old.) When this happened, they were completely amazed! But Jesus gave them strict orders not to tell anyone, and he said, "Give her something to eat."

*Jesus Sends the Apostles to Heal and Preach*

Then Jesus went to the villages round there, teaching the people. He called the twelve disciples together and sent them out two by two. He gave them authority over the evil spirits and ordered them, "Don't take anything with you on the trip except a walking stick — no bread, no beggar's bag, no money in your pockets. Wear sandals, but don't wear an extra shirt." He also told them, "Wherever you are welcomed, stay in the same house until you leave that place. If you come to a town where people do not welcome you or will not listen to you, leave it and shake the dust off your feet. That will be a warning to them."

## Jesus Feeds the Five Thousand

The apostles returned and met with Jesus, and told him all they had done and taught. There were so many people coming and going that Jesus and his disciples didn't even have time to eat. So he said to them, "Let us go off by ourselves to some place where we will be alone and you can rest a while." So they started out in the boat by themselves to a lonely place.

Many people, however, saw them leave and knew at once who they were; so they went from all the towns and ran ahead by land and arrived at the place ahead of Jesus and his disciples. When Jesus got out of the boat, he saw this large crowd, and his heart was filled with pity for them, because they were like sheep without a shepherd. So he began to teach them many things. When it was getting late, his disciples came to him and said, "It is already very late, and this is a lonely place. Send the people away, and let them go to the nearby farms and villages in order to buy themselves something to eat."

"You yourselves give them something to eat," Jesus answered.

They asked, "Do you want us to go and spend two hundred silver coins on bread in order to feed them?"

So Jesus asked them, "How much bread do you have? Go and see."

When they found out they told him, "Five loaves, and two fish also."

Jesus then told his disciples to make all the people divide into groups and sit down on the green grass. So the people sat down in rows, in groups of a hundred and groups of fifty. Then Jesus took the five loaves and the two fish, looked up to heaven, and gave thanks to God. He broke the loaves and gave them to his disciples to distribute to the people. He also divided the two fish among them all. Everyone ate and had enough. Then the disciples took up twelve baskets full of what was left of the bread and the fish. The number of men who were fed was five thousand.

## Jesus Walks on the Water

At once Jesus made his disciples get into the boat and go ahead of him to Bethsaida, on the other side of the lake, while he sent the crowd away. After saying good-bye to the people, he went away to a hill to pray. When evening came, the boat was in the middle of the lake, while Jesus was alone on land. He saw that his disciples were straining at the oars, because they were rowing against the wind; so sometime between three and six o'clock in the morning, he came to them, walking on the water. He was going to pass them by, but they saw him walking on the water. "It's a ghost" they thought, and screamed. They were all terrified when they saw him.

Jesus spoke to them at once, "Courage!" he said. "It is I. Don't be afraid!" Then he got into the boat with them, and the wind died down. The disciples were completely amazed, because they had not understood the real meaning of the feeding of the five thousand; their minds could not grasp it.

### Jesus Heals the Sick in Gennesaret

They crossed the lake and came to land at Gennesaret, where they tied up the boat. As they left the boat, people recognized Jesus at once. So they ran throughout the whole region; and wherever they heard he was, they brought to him the sick lying on their mats. And everywhere Jesus went, to villages, towns, or farms, people would take their sick to the market places and beg him to let the sick at least touch the edge of his cloak. And all who touched it were made well.

### A Woman's Faith

Then Jesus left and went away to the territory near the city of Tyre. He went into a house and did not want anyone to know he was there, but he could not stay hidden. A certain woman, whose daughter had an evil spirit in her, heard about Jesus and came to him at once and fell at his feet. The woman was a gentile, born in the region of Phoenicia of Syria. She begged Jesus to drive the demon out of her daughter. But Jesus answered, "Let us first feed the children. It isn't right to take the children's food and throw it to the dogs."

"Sir," she screamed, "even the dogs under the table eat the children's leftovers!"

So Jesus said to her, "Because of that answer, go back home where you will find that the demon has gone out of your daughter!"

She went back home and found her child lying on the bed, the demon had indeed gone out of her.

### Jesus Heals a Deaf-mute

Jesus then left the neighborhood of Tyre and went on through Sidon to Lake Galilee, going by way of the territory of the Ten Towns. Some people brought him a man who was deaf and could hardly speak, and they begged Jesus to place his hand on him. So Jesus took him off alone, away from the crowd, put his fingers in the man's ears, spat, and touched the man's tongue. Then Jesus looked up to heaven, gave a deep groan, and said to the man, "*Ephphatha,*" which means, "Open up!"

At once the man was able to hear, his speech impediment was removed, and he began to talk without any trouble. Then Jesus ordered the people not to speak of it to anyone; but the more he ordered them not to, the more they told it. And all who heard were completely amazed. "How well he does everything!" they exclaimed.

# 3
# Stories Told by Jesus

*Everyone enjoys a story. That is why Jesus taught people by telling them stories or parables. They were such good stories that they have never been forgotten. But as we read any one of them, we ought to ask: what lesson does it teach?*

*Some of these stories were parables told in order to show God's love and patience. Others were told in order to show our danger and our duty.*

## Stories about God's Love: The Lost Sheep

One day when many tax collectors and other outcasts came to listen to Jesus, the Pharisees and the teachers of the Law started grumbling, "This man welcomes outcasts and even eats with them!" So Jesus told them this parable:

"Suppose one of you has a hundred sheep and loses one of them — what does he do? He leaves the other ninety-nine sheep in the pasture and goes looking for the one that got lost until he finds it. When he finds it, he is so happy that he puts it on his shoulders, and carries it back home. Then he calls his friends and neighbors together and says to them, 'I am so happy I found my lost sheep. Let us celebrate!' In the same way, I tell you, there will be more joy in heaven over one sinner who repents than over ninety-nine respectable people who do not need to repent."

### The Parable of the Lost Coin

"Or suppose a woman who has ten silver coins loses one of them — what does she do? She lights a lamp, sweeps her house, and looks carefully everywhere until she finds it. When she finds it, she calls her friends and neighbors together, and says to them, 'I am so happy I found the coin I lost. Let us celebrate!' In the same way, I tell you, the angels of God rejoice over one sinner who repents."

## The Parable of the Lost Son

Jesus went on to say, "There was a man who had two sons. The younger one said to him, 'Father, give me my share of the property now.' So the man divided his property between his two sons. After a few days the younger son sold his part of the property and left home with the money. He went to a country far away, where he wasted his money in reckless living. He spent everything he had. Then a severe famine spread over that country, and he was left without a thing. So he went to work for one of the citizens of that country, who sent him out to his farm to take care of the pigs. He wished he could fill himself with the bean pods the pigs ate, but no one gave him anything to eat. At last he came to his senses and said, 'All my father's hired workers have more than they can eat, and here I am about to starve! I will get up and go to my father and say, "Father, I have sinned against God and against you. I am no longer fit to be called your son; treat me as one of your hired workers."' So he got up and started back to his father.

"He was still a long way from home when his father saw him; his heart was filled with pity and he ran, threw his arms around his son, and kissed him. 'Father,' the son said, 'I have sinned against God and against you. I am no longer fit to be called your son.' But the father called to his servants. 'Hurry!' he said. 'Bring the best robe and put it on him. Put a ring on his finger and shoes on his feet. Then go get the prize calf and kill it, and let us celebrate with a feast! For this son of mine was dead, but now he is alive; he was lost, but now he has been found.' And so the feasting began.

"In the meantime the older son was out in the field. On his way back, when he came close to the house, he heard the music and dancing. So he called one of the servants and asked him, 'What's going on?' 'Your brother came back home,' the servant answered, 'and your father killed the prize calf, because he got him back safe and sound.' The older brother was so angry that he would not go into the house; so his father came out and begged him to come in. 'Look, all these years I have worked for you like a slave, and I have never disobeyed your orders. What have you given me? Not even a goat for me to have a feast with my friends! But this son of yours wasted all your property on prostitutes, and when he comes back home, you kill the prize calf for him!' 'My son,' the father answered, 'You are always here with me and everything I have is yours. But we had to celebrate and be happy, because your brother was dead, but now he is alive; he was lost, but now he has been found.' "

### The Parable of the Workers in the Vineyard

"The Kingdom of heaven is like this. Once there was a man who went out early in the morning to hire some men to work in his vineyard. He agreed to pay them the regular wage, a silver coin a day, and sent them to work in his vineyard. He went out again to the market place at nine o'clock and saw some men standing there doing nothing, so he told them, 'You also go and work in the vineyard, and I will pay you a fair wage.' So they went. Then at twelve o'clock and again at three o'clock he did the same thing. It was nearly five o'clock when he went to the market place and saw some other men still standing there. 'Why are you wasting the whole day here doing nothing?' he asked them. 'No one hired us,' they answered. 'Well, then, you also go and work in the vineyard,' he told them.

"When evening came, the owner told his foreman, 'Call the workers and pay them their wages, starting with those who were hired last, and ending with those who were hired first.' The men who had begun to work at five o'clock were paid a silver coin each. So when the men who were the first to be hired came to be paid, they thought they would get more; but they too were given a silver coin each. They took their money and started grumbling against the employer. These men who were hired last worked only one hour,' they said, 'while we put up with a whole day's work in the hot sun — yet you paid them the same as you paid us!' 'Listen, friend,' the owner answered one of them. 'I have not cheated you. After all, you agreed to do a day's work for one silver coin. Now, take your pay and go home. I want to give this man who was hired last as much as I gave you. Don't I have the right to do as I wish with my own money? Or are you jealous because I am generous?' "

### The Parable of the Hidden Treasure

"The Kingdom of heaven is like this. A man happens to find a treasure hidden in a field. He covers it up again and is so happy that he goes and sells everything he has, and then goes back and buys that field."

### The Parable of the Pearl

"Also, the Kingdom of heaven is like this. A man is looking for fine pearls, and when he finds one that is unusually fine, he goes and sells everything he has, and buys that pearl."

### The Parable of the Net

"Also, the Kingdom of heaven is like this. Some fishermen throw their nets out in the lake, and catch all kinds of fish. When the net is full, they pull it to shore and sit down to divide the fish: the good ones go into the buckets, the worthless ones are thrown away. It will be like this at the end of the age: the angels will go out and gather up the evil people from among the good, and will throw them into the fiery furnace where they will cry and gnash their teeth."

*The Parable of the Storage Room*

"Do you understand these things?" Jesus asked them.

"Yes," they answered.

So he replied, "This means, then, that every teacher of the Law who becomes a disciple in the Kingdom of heaven is like a homeowner who takes new and old things out of his storage room."

## Stories about God's Patience: The Growing Seed

Jesus went on to say, "The Kingdom of God is like this. A man scatters seed in his field. He sleeps at night, is up and about during the day, and all the while the seeds are sprouting and growing. Yet he does not know how it happens. The soil itself makes the plants grow and bear fruit; first the tender stalk appears, then the head, and finally the head full of grain. When the grain is ripe, the man starts cutting it with his sickle, because harvest time has come."

*The Parable of the Sower*

Jesus began to teach beside Lake Galilee. The crowd that gathered round him was so large that he got into a boat and sat in it. The boat was out in the water, and the crowd stood on the shore, at the water's edge. He used parables to teach them many things; saying to them:

"Listen! Once there was a man who went out to sow grain. As he scattered the seed in the field, some of it fell along the path, and the birds came and ate it up. Some of it fell on rocky ground, where there was little soil. The seeds soon sprouted, because the soil wasn't deep. Then when the sun came up it burned the young plants; and because the roots had not grown deep enough, the plants soon dried up. Some of the seed fell among thorn bushes, which grew up and choked the plants, and they didn't bear grain. But some seeds fell in good soil, and the plants sprouted, grew, and bore grain: some had thirty grains, others sixty, and others one hundred."

And Jesus concluded, "Listen, then, if you have ears!"

*The Parable of the Weeds*

Jesus told them another parable: "The Kingdom of heaven is like this.

A man sowed good seed in his field. One night, when everyone was asleep, an enemy came and sowed weeds among the wheat, and went away. When the plants grew and the heads of grain began to form, then the weeds showed up. The man's servants came to him and said, 'Sir, it was good seed you sowed in your field; where did the weeds come from?' 'It was some enemy who did this,' he answered. 'Do you want us to go and pull up the weeds?' they asked him. 'No,' he answered, 'because as you gather the weeds you might pull up some of the wheat along with them. Let the wheat and the weeds both grow together until harvest. Then I will tell the harvest workers to pull up the weeds first, tie them in bundles and burn them, and then to gather in the wheat and put it in my barn.' "

### The Parable of the Mustard Seed

Jesus asked, "What is the Kingdom of God like? What shall I compare it with? It is like this. A man takes a mustard seed and plants it in his field: The plant grows and becomes a tree, and the birds make their nests in its branches."

### The Parable of the Yeast

Again Jesus asked, "What shall I compare the Kingdom of God with? It is like this. A woman takes some yeast and mixes it with a bushel of of flour until the whole batch of dough rises."

### The Lesson of the Fig Tree

Then Jesus told them this parable: "Think of the fig tree and all the other trees. When you see their leaves beginning to appear, you know that summer is near. In the same way, when you see these things happening, you will know that the Kingdom of God is about to come.

"Remember that all these things will take place before the people now living have all died. Heaven and earth will pass away, but my words will never pass away."

### The Parable of the Unfruitful Fig Tree

Then Jesus told them this parable: "There was once a man who had a fig tree growing in his vineyard. He went looking for figs on it but found none. So he said to his gardener, 'Look, for three years I have been coming here looking for figs on this fig tree and I haven't found any. Cut it down! Why should it go on using up the soil?' But the gardener answered, 'Leave it alone, sir, just one more year; I will dig round it and put in some fertilizer. Then if the tree bears figs next year, so much the better; if not, then you can have it cut down.' "

*The Parable of the Great Feast*

When one of the men sitting at the table heard this he said to Jesus, "How happy are those who will sit down at the feast in the Kingdom of God!"

Jesus said to him, "There was a man who was giving a great feast to which he invited many people. When it was time for the feast, he sent his servant to tell his guests, 'Come, everything is ready!' But they all began, one after another, to make excuses. The first one told the servant, 'I have bought a field, and must go and look at it; please accept my apologies.' Another one said, 'I have bought five pairs of oxen and am on my way to try them out; please accept my apologies.' Another one said, 'I have just gotten married, and for that reason I cannot come.' The servant went back and told all this to his master. The master was furious and said to his servant, 'Hurry out to the streets and alleys of the town, and bring back the poor, the crippled, the blind, and the lame.' Soon the servant said, 'Your order has been carried out, sir, but there is room for more.' So the master said to the servant, 'Go out to the country roads and lanes, and make people come in, so that my house will be full. I tell you all that none of those men who were invited will taste my dinner!' "

## Stories about our Danger: the Ten Girls

(Jesus is speaking of what it will be like on the day of his second coming.) At that time the Kingdom of heaven will be like this. Once there were ten girls who took their oil lamps and went out to meet the bridegroom. Five of them were foolish, and the other five were wise. The foolish ones took their lamps but did not take any extra oil with them, while the wise ones took containers full of oil for their lamps. The bridegroom was late in coming, so the girls began to nod and fall asleep.

"It was already midnight when the cry rang out. 'Here is the bridegroom! Come and meet him!' The ten girls woke up and trimmed their lamps. Then the foolish ones said to the wise ones, 'Let us have some of your oil, because our lamps are going out.' 'No, indeed,' the wise ones answered, 'there is not enough for you and for us. Go to the store and buy some for yourselves.' So the foolish girls went off to buy some oil, and while they were gone the bridegroom arrived. The five girls who were ready went in with him to the wedding feast, and the door was closed.

"Later the other girls arrived. 'Sir, sir! Let us in!' they cried out. 'Certainly not! I don't know you,' the bridegroom answered."

And Jesus concluded, "Watch out, then, because you do not know the day or hour."

*The Parable of the Three Servants*

"At that time the Kingdom of Heaven will be like this. Once there was a man who was about to leave home on a trip; he called his servants and put them in charge of his property. He gave to each one according to his ability: to one he gave five thousand silver coins, to another he gave two thousand silver coins, and to another he gave one thousand silver coins. Then he left on his trip. The servant who had received five thousand coins went at once and invested his money and earned another five thousand coins. In the same way the servant who received two thousand coins earned another two thousand coins. But the servant who received one thousand coins went off, dug a hole in the ground, and hid his master's money.

"After a long time the master of those servants came back and settled accounts with them. The servant who had received five thousand coins came in and handed over the other five thousand coins. 'You gave me five thousand coins, sir,' he said. 'Look! Here are another five thousand coins that I have earned.' 'Well done, you good and faithful servant!' said his master. 'You have been faithful in managing small amounts, so I will put you in charge of large amounts. Come on in and share my happiness!' Then the servant who had been given two thousand coins came in and said, 'You gave me two thousand coins, sir. Look! Here are another two thousand coins that I have earned.' 'Well done, you good and faithful servant!' said his master. 'You have been faithful in managing small amounts, so I will put you in charge of large amounts. Come on in and share my happiness!' Then the servant who had received one thousand coins came in and said, 'Sir, I know you are a hard man; you reap harvests where you did not plant, and you gather crops where you did not scatter seed. I was afraid, so I went off and hid your money in the ground. Look! Here is what belongs to you.' 'You bad and lazy servant!' his master said, 'You knew, did you, that I reap harvests where I did not plant, and gather crops where I did not scatter seed? Well, then, you should have deposited my money in the bank, and I would have received it all back with interest when I returned. Now, take the money away from him and give it to the one who has ten thousand coins. For to every person who has something, even more will be given, and he will have more than enough; but the person who has nothing, even the little that he has will be taken away from him. As for this useless servant — throw him outside in the darkness; there he will cry and gnash his teeth.' "

*Watchful Servants*

"Be ready for whatever comes, dressed for action and with your lamps lit, like servants who are waiting for their master to come back from a wedding feast. When he comes and knocks, they will open the door for him at once. How happy are those servants whose master finds them awake and ready when he returns! I tell you, he will take off his coat, have them sit down, and will wait on them. How happy they are if he finds them ready, even if he should come at midnight or even later! And you can be sure that if the owner of a house knew the time when the thief would come, he would not let the thief break into his house. And you, too, must be ready, because the Son of Man will come at an hour when you are not expecting him."

### The Faithful or the Unfaithful Servant

Peter said, "Lord, does this parable apply to us, or do you mean it for everyone."

The Lord answered, "Who, then, is the faithful and wise servant? He is the one that his master will put in charge, to run the household and give the other servants their share of the food at the proper time. How happy that servant is if his master finds him doing this when he comes home! Indeed, I tell you, the master will put that servant in charge of all his property. But if that servant says to himself, That his master is taking a long time to come back and if he begins to beat the other servants, both the men and the women, and eats and drinks and gets drunk, then the master will come back one day when the servant does not expect him and at a time he does not know. The master will cut him in pieces and make him share the fate of the disobedient.

"The servant who knows what his master wants him to do, but does not get himself ready and do it, will be punished with a heavy whipping. But the servant who does not know what his master wants, and yet does something for which he deserves a whipping, will be punished with a light whipping. Much is required from the person to whom much is given; much more is required from the person to whom much more is given."

### The Parable of the Rich Fool

A man in the crowd said to Jesus, "Teacher, tell my brother to divide with me the property our father left us."

Jesus answered him, "Man, who gave me the right to judge, or to divide the property between you two?" And he went on to say to them all, "Watch out and guard yourselves from every kind of greed; because a person's true life is not made up of the things he owns, no matter how rich he may be."

Then Jesus told them this parable: "There was once a rich man who had land which bore good crops. He began to think to himself, 'I don't have a place to keep all my crops. What can I do? This is what I will do,' he told himself; 'I will tear down my barns and build bigger ones, where

I will store the grain and all my other goods. Then I will say to myself, Lucky man! You have all the good things you need for many years. Take life easy, eat, drink, and enjoy yourself!' But God said to him, 'You fool! This very night you will have to give up your life; then who will get all these things you have kept for yourself?' "

And Jesus concluded, "This is how it is with those who pile up riches for themselves but are not rich in God's sight."

### The Rich Man and Lazarus

"There was once a rich man who dressed in the most expensive clothes and lived in great luxury every day. There was also a poor man named Lazarus, covered with sores, who used to be brought to the rich man's door, hoping to eat the bits of food that fell from the rich man's table. Even the dogs would come and lick his sores. The poor man died and was carried by the angels to sit beside Abraham at the feast in heaven. The rich man died and was buried, and in Hades, where he was in great pain, he looked up and saw Abraham, far away, with Lazarus at his side. So he called out, 'Father Abraham! Take pity on me, and send Lazarus to dip his finger in some water and cool off my tongue, because I am in great pain in this fire!' But Abraham said, 'Remember, my son, that in your lifetime you were given all the good things, while Lazarus got all the bad things. But now he is enjoying himself here, while you are in pain. Besides all that, there is a deep pit lying between us, so that those who want to cross over from here to you cannot do so, nor can anyone cross over to us from where you are.' The rich man said, 'Then I beg you, father Abraham, send Lazarus to my father's house, where I have five brothers. Let him go and warn them so that they, at least, will not come to this place of pain.' Abraham said, 'Your brothers have Moses and the prophets to warn them; your brothers should listen to what they say.' The rich man answered, 'That is not enough, father Abraham! But if someone were to rise from death and go to them, then they would turn from their sins.' But Abraham said, 'If they will not listen to Moses and the prophets, they will not be convinced even if someone were to rise from death.' "

### The Parable of the Tenants in the Vineyard

Then Jesus told the people this parable, "There was once a man who planted a vineyard, rented it out to tenants, and then left home for a long time. When the time came to gather the grapes, he sent a slave to the tenants to receive from them his share of the harvest. But the tenants beat the slave and sent him back without a thing. So he sent another slave; but the tenants beat him also, treated him shamefully, and sent him back

without a thing. Then he sent a third slave; the tenants wounded him, too, and threw him out. Then the owner of the vineyard said, 'What shall I do? I will send my own dear son; surely they will respect him!" But when the tenants saw him, they said to one another, 'This is the owner's son. Let's kill him, and his property will be ours!' So they threw him out of the vineyard and killed him.

"What, then, will the owner of the vineyard do to the tenants?" Jesus asked. "He will come and kill those men, and turn over the vineyard to other tenants."

### The Parable of the Unforgiving Servant

Then Peter came to Jesus and asked, "Lord, if my brother keeps on sinning against me, how many times do I have to forgive him? Seven times?"

"No, not seven times," answered Jesus, "but seventy times seven because the Kingdom of heaven is like this. Once there was a king who decided to check on his servants' accounts. He had just begun to do so when one of them was brought in who owed him millions of dollars. The servant did not have enough to pay his debt, so the king ordered him to be sold as a slave, with his wife and his children and all that he had, in order to pay the debt. The servant fell on his knees before the king. 'Be patient with me,' he begged, 'and I will pay you everything!' The king felt sorry for him, so he forgave him the debt and let him go.

"Then the man went out and met one of his fellow servants who owed him a few dollars. He grabbed him and started choking him. 'Pay back what you owe me!' he said. His fellow servant fell down and begged him, 'Be patient with me and I will pay you back!' But he refused; instead, he had him thrown into jail until he should pay the debt. When the other servants saw what had happened, they were very upset, and went to the king and told him everything. So he called the servant in. 'You worthless slave!' he said. 'I forgave you the whole amount you owed me, just because you asked me to. You should have had mercy on your fellow servant, just as I had mercy on you.' The king was very angry, and he sent the servant to jail to be punished until he should pay back the whole amount."

And Jesus concluded, "That is how my Father in heaven will treat every one of you unless you forgive your brother, from your heart."

### The Parable of the Two Sons

"Now, what do you think? There was once a man who had two sons. He went to the older one and said, 'Son, go and work in the vineyard today.' 'I don't want to,' he answered, but later he changed his mind and went. Then the father went to the other son and said the same thing.

'Yes, sir,' he answered, but he did not go. Which one of the two did what his father wanted?"

"The older one," they answered.

"So Jesus said to them, I tell you: the tax collectors and the prostitutes are going into the Kingdom of God ahead of you. For John the Baptist came to you showing you the right path to take, and you would not believe him; but the tax collectors and the prostitutes believed him. Even when you saw this, you did not later change your minds and believe him."

## The Return of the Evil Spirit

"When an evil spirit goes out of a person, it travels over dry country looking for a place to rest. If it can't find one, it says to itself, 'I will go back to my house.' So it goes back and finds the house clean and all fixed up. Then it goes out and brings seven other spirits even worse than itself, and they come and live there. So when it is all over, that person is in worse shape than he was at the beginning."

## Stories about our Duty

### The Parable of the Widow and the Judge

Then Jesus told his disciples a parable to teach them that they should always pray and never become discouraged. "In a certain town there was a judge who neither feared God nor respected man. And there was a widow in that same town who kept coming to him and pleading for her rights, saying, 'Help me against my opponent!' For a long time the judge refused to act, but at last he said to himself, "Even though I don't fear God or respect man, yet because of all the trouble this widow is giving me, I will see to it that she gets her rights. If I don't she will keep on coming and finally wear me out!' "

And the Lord continued, "Listen to what that corrupt judge said. Now, will God not judge in favor of his own people who cry to him day and night for help? Will he be slow to help them? I tell you, he will judge in their favor, and do it quickly. But will the Son of Man find faith on earth when he comes?"

### The Parable of the Friend at Midnight

And Jesus said to his disciples, "Suppose one of you should go to a friend's house at midnight and say to him, 'Friend, let me borrow three loaves of bread. A friend of mine who is on a trip has just come to my house and I don't have any food for him! And suppose your friend should answer from inside, 'Don't bother me! The door is already locked, and my children and I are in bed. I can't get up and give you anything.'

Well, what then? I tell you that even if he will not get up and give you the bread because you are his friend, yet he will get up and give you everything you need because you are not ashamed to keep on asking."

## The Parable of the Pharisee and the Tax Collector

Jesus also told this parable to people who were sure of their own goodness and despised everybody else. "Once there were two men who went up to the Temple to pray; one was a Pharisee, the other a tax collector. The Pharisee stood apart by himself and prayed, 'I thank you, God, that I am not greedy, dishonest, or an adulterer, like everybody else. I thank you that I am not like that tax collector over there. I fast two days a week, and I give you one tenth of all my income.' But the tax collector stood at a distance and would not even raise his face to heaven, but beat on his breast and said, 'God, have pity on me, a sinner!' I tell you," said Jesus, "the tax collector and not the Pharisee, was in the right with God when he went home. For everyone who makes himself great will be humbled, and everyone who humbles himself will be made great."

## The Parable of the Good Samaritan

A teacher of the Law came up and tried to trap Jesus. "Teacher," he asked, "what must I do to receive eternal life?"

Jesus answered him, "What do the Scriptures say? How do you interpret them?"

The man answered, "Love the Lord your God with all your heart, with all your soul, with all your strength, and with all your mind; and, 'Love your neighbor as you love yourself.' "

"You are right," Jesus replied; "do this and you will live."

But the teacher of the Law wanted to justify himself, so he asked Jesus, "Who is my neighbor?"

Jesus answered, "There was once a man who was going down from Jerusalem to Jericho when robbers attacked him, stripped him, and beat him up, leaving him half dead. It so happened that a priest was going down that road; but when he saw the man, he walked on by on the other side. In the same way a Levite also came there, went over and looked at the man, and then walked on by on the other side. But a Samaritan who was traveling that way came upon the man, and when he saw him, his heart was filled with pity. He went over to him, poured oil and wine on his wounds and bandaged them; then he put the man on his own animal and took him to an inn, where he took care of him. The next day he took out two silver coins and gave them to the innkeeper. "Take care of him,' he told the innkeeper, 'and when I come back this way I will pay you whatever you spend on him.' "

And Jesus concluded, "In your opinion, which one of these three acted like a neighbor toward the man attacked by the robbers?"

The teacher of the Law answered, "The one who was kind to him."

Jesus replied, "You go, then, and do the same."

## The Final Judgment

"When the Son of Man comes as King and all the angels with him, he will sit on his royal throne, and the people of all the nations will be gathered before him. Then he will divide them into two groups, just as a shepherd separates the sheep from the goats. He will put the righteous people at his right and the others at his left. Then the King will say to the people on his right, 'Come, you are blessed by my Father! Come and possess the kingdom which has been prepared for you ever since the creation of the world. I was hungry and you fed me, thirsty and you gave me a drink; I was a stranger and you received me in your homes, naked and you clothed me; I was sick and you took care of me, in prison and you visited me.' The righteous will then answer him, 'When, Lord, did we ever see you hungry and feed you, or thirsty and give you a drink? When did we ever see you a stranger and welcome you in our homes, or naked and clothe you? When did we ever see you sick or in prison, and visit you?' The King will reply, 'I tell you, indeed, whenever you did this for one of the least important of these brothers of mine, you did it for me!'

"Then he will say to those on his left, 'Away from me, you that are under God's curse! Away to the eternal fire which has been prepared for the Devil and his angels! I was hungry but you would not feed me, thirsty but you would not give me drink; I was a stranger but you would not welcome me in your homes, naked but you would not clothe me; I was sick and in prison but you would not take care of me.' Then they will answer him, 'When, Lord, did we ever see you hungry or thirsty or a stranger or naked or sick or in prison, and we would not help you?' The King will reply, 'I tell you, whenever you refused to help one of these least important ones, you refused to help me.' These, then, will be sent off to eternal punishment, but the righteous will go to eternal life."

# 4
# Jesus Teaches

*Matthew has given us much of the teaching of Jesus in the Sermon on the Mount. This shows how Jesus' followers ought to live, knowing that God is their Father and King.*

*But Jesus said many other things while he was teaching. He warned people against many of the teachers of the religious Law and the Pharisees. These Pharisees were proud because they obeyed all the religious Law, and they despised ordinary people. Jesus called them hypocrites, a word which means actors in a play. They were just acting. But it is important to remember that Jesus was not criticizing Jewish teachers only, and that many Christians have been hypocrites.*

## The Sermon on the Mount

Jesus saw the crowds and went up a hill, where he sat down. His disciples gathered round him, and he began to teach them:

*True Happiness*

"Happy are those who know they are spiritually poor;
   the Kingdom of heaven belongs to them!
"Happy are those who mourn;
   God will comfort them!
"Happy are those who are humble;
   they will receive what God has promised!
"Happy are those whose greatest desire is to do what God
      requires;
   God will satisfy them fully!
"Happy are those who are merciful to others;
   God will be merciful to them!
"Happy are the pure in heart;
   they will see God!
"Happy are those who work for peace among men;
   God will call them his children!
"Happy are those who are persecuted because they do what
      God requires;
   the Kingdom of heaven belongs to them!
"Happy are you when people insult you, and persecute you, and tell all

kinds of evil lies against you because you are my followers. Be happy and glad, for a great reward is kept for you in heaven. This is how the prophets who lived before you were persecuted."

## Salt and Light

"You are like salt for all mankind. But if salt loses its saltiness, there is no way to make it salty again. It has become worthless, so it is thrown out and people trample on it.

"You are like light for the whole world. A city built on a hill cannot be hid. No one lights a lamp and puts it under a bowl; instead he puts it on the lampstand, where it gives light for everyone in the house. In the same way your light must shine before people, so that they will see the good things you do and praise to your Father in heaven."

## Teaching about the Law

"Do not think that I have come to do away with the Law of Moses and the teachings of the prophets. I have not come to do away with them, but to make their teachings come true. Remember that as long as heaven and earth last, not the least point nor the smallest detail of the Law

will be done away with — not until the end of all things. So then, whoever disobeys even the least important of the commandments and teaches others to do the same, will be least in the Kingdom of heaven. On the other hand, whoever obeys the Law and teaches others to do the same, will be great in the Kingdom of heaven. I tell you, then, that you will be able to enter the Kingdom of heaven only if you are more faithful than the teachers of the Law and the Pharisees in doing what God requires."

## Teaching about Anger

"You have heard that people were told in the past, 'Do not commit murder; anyone who does will be brought to trial.' But now I tell you: whoever is angry with his brother will be brought to trial, whoever calls his brother 'You good-for-nothing!' will be brought before the Council, and whoever calls his brother a worthless fool will be in danger of going to the fire of hell. So if you are about to offer your gift to God at the altar and there you remember that your brother has something against you, leave your gift there in front of the altar, go at once and make peace with your brother, then come back and offer your gift to God.

"If someone brings a lawsuit against you and takes you to court, settle the dispute with him while there is time, before you get to court. Once you are there, he will turn you over to the judge, who will hand you over to the police, and you will be put in jail. There you will stay, I tell you, until you pay the last penny of your fine."

## Teaching about Adultery

"You have heard that it was said, 'Do not commit adultery.' But now I tell you: anyone who looks at a woman and wants to possess her is guilty of committing adultery with her in his heart. So if your right eye causes you to sin, take it out and throw it away! It is much better for you to lose a part of your body than to have your whole body thrown into hell. If your right hand causes you to sin, cut it off and throw it away! It is much better for you to lose one of your limbs than to have your whole body go off to hell."

## Teaching about Divorce

"It was also said, 'Anyone who divorces his wife must give her a written notice of divorce.' But now I tell you: if a man divorces his wife, even though she has not been unfaithful, then he is guilty of making her commit adultery if she marries again; and the man who marries her commits adultery also."

66

*Teaching about Vows*

"You have also heard that people were told in the past, 'Do not break your promise, but do what you have vowed to the Lord to do.' But now I tell you: do not use any vow when you make a promise. Do not swear by heaven, because it is God's throne; nor by earth, because it is the resting place for his feet; nor by Jerusalem, because it is the city of the great King. Do not even swear by your head, because you cannot make a single hair white or black. Just say 'Yes' or 'No' — anything else you say comes from the Evil One."

*Teaching about Revenge*

"You have heard that it was said, 'An eye for an eye, and a tooth for a tooth.' But now I tell you: do not take revenge on someone who wrongs you. If anyone slaps you on the right cheek, let him slap your left cheek too. And if someone takes you to court to sue you for your shirt, let him have your coat as well. And if one of the occupation troops forces you to carry his pack one mile, carry it two miles. When someone asks you for something, give it to him; when someone wants to borrow something, lend it to him."

*Love for Enemies*

"You have heard that it was said, 'Love your friends, hate your enemies.' 'But now I tell you: love your enemies, and pray for those who persecute you, so that you may become the sons of your Father in heaven. For he makes his sun to shine on bad and good people alike, and gives rain to those who do good and those who do evil. Why should God reward you if you love only the people who love you? Even the tax collectors do that! And if you speak only to your friends, have you done anything out of the ordinary? Even the pagans do that! You must be perfect — just as your Father in heaven is perfect."

*Teaching about Charity*

"Make certain you do not perform your religious duties in public so that people will see what you do. If you do these things publicly you will not have any reward from your Father in heaven."

"So when you give something to a needy person, do not make a big show of it, as the hypocrites do in the houses of worship and on the streets. They do it so that people will praise them. I assure you, they have already been paid in full. But when you help a needy person, do it in such a way that even your closest friend will not know about it. Then it will be a private matter. And your Father, who sees what you do in private, will reward you."

*Teaching about Prayer*

"When you pray, do not be like the hypocrites! They love to stand up and pray in the houses of worship and on the street corners so that everyone will see them. I assure you, they have already been paid in full. But when you pray, go to your room, close the door, and pray to your Father, who is unseen. And your Father, who sees what you do in private, will reward you.

"When you pray do not use a lot of meaningless words, as the pagans do, who think that God will hear them because their prayers are long. Do not be like them. Your Father already knows what you need before you ask him. This, then, is how you should pray:
'Our Father in heaven:
May your holy name be honored;
may your kingdom come;
may your will be done on earth as it is in heaven.
Give us today the food we need.
Forgive us the wrongs that we have done, as we forgive the
    wrongs that others have done us.
Do not bring us to hard testing,
    but keep us safe from the Evil One.' "

*Teaching about Forgiveness*

"If you forgive others the wrongs they have done to you, your Father in heaven will also forgive you. But if you do not forgive others, then your Father will not forgive the wrongs you have done."

*Teaching about Fasting*

"And when you fast, do not put on a sad face as the hypocrites do. They neglect their appearance so that everyone will see that they are fasting. I assure you, they have already been paid in full. When you go without food, wash your face and comb your hair, so that others cannot know that you are fasting — only your Father, who is unseen, will know. And your Father, who sees what you do in private, will reward you."

*Riches in Heaven*

"Do not save riches for yourselves here on earth, where moths and rust destroy, and robbers break in and steal. Instead, store up riches for yourselves in heaven, where moths and rust cannot destroy, and robbers cannot break in and steal. For your heart will always be where your riches are."

*The Light of the Body*

"The eyes are like a lamp for the body. If your eyes are sound, your

68

whole body will be full of light; but if your eyes are no good, your body will be in darkness. So if the light in you is darkness, how terribly dark it will be!"

## God and Possessions

"No one can be a slave to two masters; he will hate one and love the other; he will be loyal to one and despise the other. You cannot serve both God and money.

"This is why I tell you: do not be worried about the food and drink you need in order to stay alive, or about clothes for your body. After all, isn't life worth more than food? And isn't the body worth more than clothes? Look at the birds flying around: they do not plant seeds, gather a harvest, and put it in barns; your Father in heaven takes care of them! Aren't you worth much more than birds? Can any of you live a bit longer by worrying about it?

"And why worry about clothes? Look how the wild flowers grow: they do not work or make clothes for themselves. But I tell you that not even King Solomon with all his wealth had clothes as beautiful as one of these flowers. It is God who clothes the wild grass — grass that is here today and gone tomorrow, burned up in the oven. Won't he be all the more sure to clothe you? How little faith you have!

"So do not start worrying: 'Where will my food come from? or my drink? or my clothes?' (These are the things the pagans are always concerned about.) Your Father in heaven knows that you need all these things. Instead, be concerned above everything else with the Kingdom of God and with what he requires of you, and he will provide you with all these other things. So do not worry about tomorrow; it will have enough worries of its own. There is no need to add to the troubles each day brings."

## Judging Others

"Do not judge others, so that God will not judge you for God will judge you in the same way you judge others, and he will apply to you the same rules you apply to others. Why, then, do you look at the speck in your brothers eye and pay no attention to the log in your own eye? How dare you say to your brother, 'Please, let me take that speck out of your eye,' when you have a log in your own eye? You hypocrite! First take the log out of your own eye, and then you will be able to see clearly to take the speck out of your brother's eye.

"Do not give what is holy to dogs — they will only turn and attack you. Do not throw your pearls in front of pigs — they will only trample them underfoot."

*Ask, Seek, Knock*

"Ask, and you will receive; seek, and you will find; knock, and the door will be opened to you. For everyone who asks will receive, and anyone who seeks will find, and the door will be opened to him who knocks. Would any of you who are fathers give your son a stone when he asks you for bread? Or would you give him a snake when he asks you for fish? As bad as you are, you know how to give good things to your children. How much more, then, will your Father in heaven give good things to those who ask him!

"Do for others what you want them to do for you: this is the meaning of the Law of Moses and of the teaching of the prophets."

*The Narrow Gate*

"Go in through the narrow gate, because the gate to hell is wide and the road that leads to it is easy and there are many who travel it. But the gate to life is narrow and the way that leads to it is hard, and there are few people who find it."

*A Tree and its Fruit*

"Be on your guard against false prophets; they come to you looking like sheep on the outside, but on the inside they are really like wild wolves. You will know them by what they do. Thorn bushes do not bear grapes, and briers do not bear figs. A healthy tree bears good fruit, but a poor tree bears bad fruit. A healthy tree cannot bear bad fruit, and a poor tree cannot bear good fruit. Any tree that does not bear good fruit is cut down and thrown in the fire. So then, you will know the false prophets by what they do."

*I Never Knew You*

"Not everyone who calls me 'Lord, Lord' will enter the Kingdom of heaven, but only those who do what my Father in heaven wants them to do. When the Judgement Day comes, many will say to me, 'Lord, Lord! In your name we spoke God's message, by your name we drove out many demons and performed many miracles!' Then I will say to them, 'I never knew you, get away from me, you wicked people!'"

*The Two House Builders*

"So then, anyone who hears these words of mine and obeys them is like a wise man who built his house on rock. The rain poured down, the rivers flooded over, and the winds blew hard against that house. But it did not fall, because it was built on rock.

"But everyone who hears these words of mine and does not obey them is like a foolish man who built his house on sand. The rain poured down, the rivers flooded over, the winds blew hard against that house, and it fell. And what a terrible fall that was!"

*The Authority of Jesus*

When Jesus finished saying these things, the crowd was amazed at the way he taught. He wasn't like the teachers of the Law; instead, he taught with authority.

## Some Other Teaching Given by Jesus

*Whom to Fear*

"So do not be afraid of people. Whatever is now covered up will be uncovered, and every secret will be made known. What I am telling you in the dark you must repeat in broad daylight, and what you have heard in private you must announce from the housetops. Do not be afraid of those who kill the body but cannot kill the soul; rather be afraid of God, who can destroy both body and soul in hell. For only a penny can buy two sparrows, yet not one sparrow falls to the ground without your Father's consent. As for you, even the hairs of your head have all been counted. So do not be afraid; you are worth much more than many sparrows!"

*Who Belongs*

"If anyone declares publicly that he belongs to me, I will do the same for him before my Father in heaven. But if anyone rejects me publicly, I will reject him before my Father in heaven."

*Not Peace, but a Sword*

Do not think that I have come to bring peace to the world: No, I did not come to bring peace, but a sword. I came to set sons against their fathers, daughters against their mothers, daughters-in-law against their mothers-in-law; a man's worst enemies will be the members of his own family.

"Whoever loves his father or mother more than me is not fit to be my disciple; whoever loves his son or daughter more than me is not fit to be my disciple. Whoever does not take up his cross and follow in my steps is not fit to be my disciple. Whoever tries to gain his own life will lose it; whoever loses his life for my sake will gain it.

"Whoever welcomes you, welcomes me; and whoever welcomes me, welcomes the one who sent me. Whoever welcomes God's messenger because he is God's messenger will share in his reward. And whoever welcomes a good man because he is good, will share in his reward. You can be sure that whoever gives even a drink of cold water to one of the least of these my followers because he is my follower, will certainly receive a reward."

### Come to Me and Rest

"Come to me, all of you who are tired from carrying heavy loads, and I will give you rest. Take my yoke and put it on you, and learn from me, because I am gentle and humble in spirit; and you will find rest. For the yoke I will give you is easy, and the load I will put on you is light."

### The Question about Paying Taxes

The Pharisees went off and made a plan to trap Jesus with questions. Then they sent to him some of their disciples and some members of Herod's party. "Teacher," they said, "we know that you tell the truth. You teach the truth about God's will for man, without worrying about what people think, because you pay no attention to a man's status. Tell us, then, what do you think? Is it against our Law to pay taxes to the Roman Emperor, or not?

Jesus, however, was aware of their evil plan, and so he said, "You hypocrites! Why are you trying to trap me? Show me the coin for paying the tax!"

They brought him the coin, and he asked them, "Whose face and name are these?"

"The Emperor's," they answered.

So Jesus said to them, "Well, then, pay to the Emperor what belongs to the Emperor, and pay God what belongs to God."

When they heard this, they were amazed; and they left him and went away.

### The Question about Rising from Death

That same day some Sadducees came to Jesus and claimed that people will not rise from death. "Teacher," they said, "Moses said that if a man has no children dies, his brother must marry the widow so they can have children who will be considered the dead man's children. Now, there were seven brothers who used to live here. The oldest got married and died without having children, so he left his widow to his brother. The same thing happened to the second brother, to the third, and finally to all seven. Last of all, the woman died. Now, on the day when the dead rise to life, whose wife will she be? All of them had married her."

Jesus answered them, "How wrong you are! It is because you don't know the Scriptures or God's power. For when the dead rise to life they will be like the angels in heaven and will not marry. Now, as for the dead rising to life: haven't you ever read what God has told you? He said, I am the God of Abraham, the God of Isaac, and the God of Jacob.' He is the God of the living, not of the dead."

When the crowds heard this they were amazed at his teaching.

### The Great Commandment

When the Pharisees heard that Jesus had silenced the Sadducees, they came together, and one of them, a teacher of the Law, tried to trap him with a question. "Teacher," he asked, "which is the greatest commandment in the Law?"

Jesus answered, " 'Love the Lord your God with all your heart, with all your soul, and with all your mind.' This is the greatest and the most important commandment. The second most important commandment is like it: 'Love your neighbor as you love yourself.' The whole Law of Moses and the teachings of the prophets depend on these two commandments."

## Jesus Warns about Hypocrisy

### Jesus Warns against the Teachers of the Law and the Pharisees

Then Jesus spoke to the crowds and to his disciples. "The teachers of the Law and the Pharisees are the authorized interpreters of Moses' Law. So you must obey and follow everything they tell you to do; do not, however, imitate their actions, because they don't practice what they preach. They tie onto people's backs loads that are heavy and hard to carry, yet they aren't willing even to lift a finger to help them carry those loads. They do everything so that people will see them. Look at the straps with scripture verses on them which they wear on their foreheads and arms, and notice how large they are. Notice also how long are the tassels on their cloaks! They love the best places at feasts and the reserved seats in the synagogues; they love to be greeted with respect in the market places and have people call them "Teacher.' You must not be called 'Teacher,' because you are all brothers of one another and have only one Teacher. And you must not call anyone here on earth 'Father,' because you have only the one Father in heaven. Nor should you be called 'Leader,' because your one and only leader is the Messiah. The greatest one among you must be your servant. Whoever makes himself great will be humbled, and whoever humbles himself will be made great."

### Jesus Condemns their Hypocrisy

"How terrible for you, teachers of the Law and Pharisees! You hypocrites!

You lock the door to the Kingdom of heaven in people's faces, but you yourselves don't go in, nor do you allow in those who are trying to enter!

"How terrible for you, teachers of the Law and Pharisees! You hypocrites! You sail the seas and cross whole countries to win one convert; and when you succeed, you make him twice as deserving of going to hell as you yourselves are!

"How terrible for you, blind guides! You teach, 'If someone swears by the Temple, he isn't bound by his vow; but if he swears by the gold in the Temple, he is bound.' Blind fools! Which is more important, the gold or the Temple which makes the gold holy? You also teach, 'If someone swears by the altar he isn't bound by his vow; but if he swears by the gift on the altar, he is bound.' How blind you are! Which is more important, the gift or the altar which makes the gift holy? So then, when a person swears by the altar, he is swearing by it and by all gifts on it; and when he swears by the Temple he is swearing by it and by God, who lives there; and when someone swears by heaven, he is swearing by God's throne and by him who sits on it.

"How terrible for you, teachers of the Law and Pharisees! You hypocrites! You give to God one tenth even of the seasoning herbs, such as mint, dill, and cumin, but you neglect to obey the really important teachings of the Law, such as justice and mercy and honesty. These you should practice, without neglecting the others. Blind guides! You strain a fly out of your drink, but swallow a camel!"

"How terrible for you, teachers of the Law and Pharisees! You hypocrites! You clean the outside of your cup and plate, while the inside is full of what you have got by violence and selfishness. Blind Pharisee! Clean what is inside the cup first, and then the outside will be clean too!

"How terrible for you, teachers of the Law and Pharisees! You hypocrites! You are like whitewashed tombs, which look fine on the outside but are full of bones and decaying corpses on the inside. In the same way, on the outside you appear good to everybody, but inside you are full of hypocrisy and sins."

## The Things that Make a Person Unclean

Then Jesus called the crowd to him and said to them, "Listen and understand! It is not what goes into a person's mouth that makes him ritually unclean; rather, what comes out of it makes him unclean."

Then the disciples came to him and said, "Do you know that the Pharisees had their feelings hurt by what you said?"

"Every plant which my Father in heaven did not plant will be pulled up," answered Jesus. "Don't worry about them! They are blind leaders of the blind; and when one blind man leads another, both fall into a ditch."

Peter spoke up, "Explain this saying to us."

Jesus said to them, "You are still no more intelligent than the others. Don't you understand? Anything that goes into a person's mouth goes into his stomach and then on out of the body. But the things that come out of the mouth come from the heart and these are the things that make a person ritually unclean. For from his heart come the evil ideas which lead him to kill, commit adultery, and do other immoral things; to rob, lie, and slander others. These are the things that make a man unclean. But to eat without washing your hands as they say you should — this doesn't make a man unclean."

# 5

# The Road to the Cross

*What Jesus taught by living was as important as what he taught by speaking. He taught us to be brave, although, after his cousin John the Baptist was killed, he saw clearly that he, too, would have to die for he, too, was doing God's work. He taught us to be humble, because he himself humbly did what God asked him to do. As he said, he did not come to be served; he came to serve.*

*So he entered Jerusalem and taught in its temple.*

## The Death of John the Baptist

King Herod heard about Jesus' reputation, which had spread everywhere. Some people were saying "John the Baptist has come back to life! That is why he has this power to perform miracles."

Others, however, said, "He is Elijah."

Others said, "He is a prophet, like one of the prophets of long ago."

When Herod heard it, he said, "He is John the Baptist! I had his head cut off, but he has come back to life!" Herod himself had ordered John's arrest, and had him tied up and put in prison. Herod did this because of Herodias, whom he had married, even though she was the wife of his brother Philip. John the Baptist kept telling Herod, "It isn't right for you to marry your brother's wife!"

So Herodias held a grudge against John and wanted to kill him, but she could not because of Herod. Herod was afraid of John because he knew that John was a good and holy man, and so he kept him safe. He liked to listen to him, even though he became greatly disturbed every time he heard him.

Finally Herodias got her chance. It was on Herod's birthday, when he gave a feast for all the top government officials, the military chiefs, and the leading citizens of Galilee. The daughter of Herodias came in and danced, and pleased Herod and his guests. So the king said to the girl, "What would you like to have? I will give you anything you want." With many vows he said to her, "I swear that I will give you anything you ask for, even as much as half my kingdom!"

So the girl went out and asked her mother, "What shall I ask for?"

"The head of John the Baptist," she answered.

The girl hurried back at once to the king and demanded, "I want you to give me here and now the head of John the Baptist on a plate!"

This made the king very sad, but he could not refuse her because of the vows he had made in front of all his guests. So he sent off a guard at once with orders to bring John's head. The guard left, went to the prison, and cut John's head off; then he brought it on a plate and gave it to the girl, who gave it to her mother. When John's disciples heard about this, they came and got his body, and laid it in a grave.

## Jesus Sees that he Must Die

*Peter's Declaration about Jesus*

Jesus went to the territory near the town of Caesarea Philippi, where he asked his disciples, "Who do people say the Son of Man is?"

"Some say John the Baptist," they answered. "Others say Elijah, while others say Jeremiah or some other prophet."

"What about you?" he asked them. "Who do you say I am?"

Simon Peter answered, "You are the Messiah, the Son of the living God."

"Good for you, Simon, son of John!" answered Jesus. "For this truth did not come to you from any human being, but it was given to you directly by my Father in heaven. And so I tell you Peter: you are a rock, and on this rock foundation I will build my church, and not even death will ever be able to overcome it. I will give you the keys of the Kingdom of heaven; what you prohibit on earth will be prohibited in heaven, what you permit on earth will be permitted in heaven."

Then Jesus ordered his disciples not to tell anyone that he was the Messiah.

*Jesus Speaks about his Suffering and Death*

Then Jesus began to teach his disciples: "The Son of Man must suffer much, and be rejected by the elders, the chief priests, and the teachers of the Law. He will be put to death, but three days later he will rise to life." He made this very clear to them. So Peter took him aside and began to rebuke him. But Jesus turned around, looked at his disciples, and rebuked Peter. "Get away from me, Satan," he said. "Your thoughts don't come from God but from man!"

Then Jesus called the crowd and his disciples to him. "If anyone wants to come with me," he told them, "he must forget himself, carry his cross, and follow me. For whoever wants to save his own life will lose it; but whoever loses his life for me and for the gospel will save it. Does a person gain anything if he wins the whole world but loses his life? Of course not! There is nothing he can give to regain his life. If a person is ashamed of me and of my teaching in this godless and wicked day, then the Son of Man will be ashamed of him when he comes in the glory of his Father with the holy angels."

And he went on to say, "I tell you there are some here who will not die until they have seen the kingdom of God come with power."

## *The Transfiguration*

Six days later Jesus took with him Peter, James, and John, and led them up a high mountain, where they were alone. As they looked on, a change came over Jesus, and his clothes became shining white — whiter than anyone in the world could wash them. Then the three disciples saw Elijah and Moses talking with Jesus. Peter spoke up and said to Jesus, "Teacher, how good it is that we are here! We will make three tents, one for you, one for Moses, and one for Elijah." He and the others were so frightened that he did not know what to say.

Then a cloud appeared and covered them with its shadow, and a voice came from the cloud, "This is my own dear Son — listen to him!" They took a quick look round but did not see anyone else; only Jesus was with them.

As they came down the mountain, Jesus ordered them, "Don't tell anyone what you have seen, until the Son of Man has risen from death."

They obeyed his order, but among themselves they started discussing the matter, "What does this 'rising from death' mean?" And they asked Jesus, "Why do the teachers of the Law say that Elijah has to come first?

His answer was, "Elijah is indeed coming first in order to get everything ready. Yet why do the Scriptures say that the Son of Man will suffer much and be rejected? I tell you, however, that Elijah has already come and that people treated him just as they pleased, as the Scriptures say about him."

## Jesus Teaches Humility

### *Who Is the Greatest?*

They came to Capernaum, and after going indoors Jesus asked his disciples, "What were you arguing about on the road?"

But they would not answer him, because on the road they had been arguing among themselves about who was the greatest. Jesus sat down, called the twelve disciples, and said to them, "Whoever wants to be first must place himself last of all and be the servant of all." Then he took a child and had him stand in front of them. He put his arms round him and said to them, "Whoever welcomes in my name one of these children, welcomes me; and whoever welcomes me, welcomes not only me but also the one who sent me."

*Who Is not against Us Is for Us*

John said to him, "Teacher, we saw a man who was driving out demons in your name, and we told him to stop, because he doesn't belong to our group."

"Do not try to stop him," Jesus told them, "because no one who performs a miracle in my name will be able soon after to say evil things about me. For whoever is not against us is for us. I assure you that anyone who gives you a drink of water because you belong to me will certainly receive his reward."

*Jesus Blesses Little Children*

Some people brought children to Jesus for him to place his hands on them, but the disciples scolded the people. When Jesus noticed this he was angry and said to his disciples, "Let the children come to me, and do not stop them, because the Kingdom of God belongs to such as these. I assure you that whoever does not receive the Kingdom of God like a child will never enter it." Then he took the children in his arms, placed his hands on each of them, and blessed them.

*The Rich Man*

As Jesus was starting on his way again, a man ran up, knelt before him and asked him, "Good Teacher, what must I do to receive eternal life?"

"Why do you call me good?" Jesus asked him. "No one is good except God alone. You know the commandments: 'Do not commit murder; do not commit adultery; do not steal; do not accuse anyone falsely; do not cheat; respect your father and your mother.'"

"Teacher," the man said, "ever since I was young I have obeyed all these commandments."

Jesus looked straight at him with love and said, "You need only one thing. Go and sell all you have and give the money to the poor, and you will have riches in heaven; then come and follow me." When the man heard this, gloom spread over his face, and he went away sad, because he was very rich.

Jesus looked round at his disciples and said to them, "How hard it will be for rich people to enter the Kingdom of God!"

The disciples were shocked at these words, but Jesus went on to say, "My children, how hard it is to enter the Kingdom of God! It is much harder for a rich person to enter the Kingdom of God than for a camel to go through the eye of a needle."

*A Samaritan Village Refuses to Receive Jesus*

As the time drew near when Jesus would be taken up to heaven, he

made up his mind and set out on his way to Jerusalem. He sent messengers ahead of him, who went into a village in Samaria to get everything ready for him. But the people there would not receive him, because it was clear that he was on his way to Jerusalem. When the disciples James and John saw this; they said, "Lord, do you want us to call fire down from heaven to destroy them?"

Jesus turned and rebuked them. Then Jesus and his disciples went on to another village.

### The Would-be Followers of Jesus

As they went on their way, a certain man said to Jesus, "I will follow you wherever you go."

Jesus said to him, "Foxes have holes, and birds have nests, but the Son of Man has no place to lie down and rest."

He said to another man, "Follow me."

But that man said, "Sir, first let me go back and bury my father."

Jesus answered, "Let the dead bury their own dead. You go and proclaim the Kingdom of God."

Another man said, "I will follow you, sir; but first let me go and say goodbye to my family."

Jesus said to him, "Anyone who starts to plow and then keeps looking back is of no use for the Kingdom of God."

### Jesus Sends out the Seventy-two

After this the Lord chose another seventy-two men and sent them out, two by two, to go ahead of him to every town and place where he himself was about to go. He said to them, "There is a large harvest, but few workers to gather it in. Pray to the owner of the harvest that he will send out workers to gather in his harvest. Go! I am sending you like lambs among wolves. Don't take a purse, or a beggar's bag or shoes; don't stop to greet anyone on the road. Whenever you go into a house, first say, 'Peace be with this house.' If a peace-loving man lives there, let your greeting of peace remain on him; if not, take back your greeting of peace. Stay in that same house, eating and drinking what they offer you, for a worker should be given his pay. Don't move round from one house to another. Whenever you go into a town and are made welcome, eat what is set before you, heal the sick in that town, and say to the people there, 'The Kingdom of God has come near you.' But whenever you go into a town and are not welcomed there, go out in the streets and say, 'Even the dust from your town that sticks to our feet we wipe off against you. But remember that the Kingdom of God has come near you!' I assure you that on the Judgment Day God will show more mercy to Sodom than to that town!"

## The Unbelieving Towns

"How terrible it will be for you, Chorazin! How terrible for you too, Bethsaida! If the miracles which were performed in you had been performed in Tyre and Sidon, the people there would have long ago sat down, put on sackcloth, and sprinkled ashes on themselves, to show that they had turned from their sins! God will show more mercy on the Judgment Day to Tyre and Sidon than to you. And as for you, Capernaum! Do you want to lift yourself up to heaven? You will be thrown down to hell!

Jesus said to his disciples, "Whoever listens to you, listens to me; whoever rejects you, rejects me; and whoever rejects me, rejects the one who sent me."

## The Return of the Seventy-two

The seventy-two men came back in great joy. "Lord," they said, "even the demons obeyed us when we command in your name!"

Jesus answered them, "I saw Satan fall like lightning from heaven. Listen! I have given you authority, so that you can walk on snakes and scorpions and overcome all the power of the Enemy, and nothing will hurt you. But don't be glad because the evil spirits obey you; rather be glad because your names are written in heaven."

At that time Jesus was filled with joy by the Holy Spirit and said, "Father, Lord of heaven and earth! I thank you because you have shown to the unlearned what you have hidden from the wise and learned. Yes, Father, this was how you were pleased to have it happen.

"My Father has given me all things. No one knows who the Son is except the Father, and no one knows who the Father is except the Son and those to whom the Son chooses to reveal him."

Then Jesus turned to the disciples and said to them privately, "How fortunate you are to see the things you see! I tell you that many prophets and Kings wanted to see what you see, but they could not, and to hear what you hear, but they did not."

## Jesus Heals a Sick Man

One Sabbath Jesus went to eat a meal at the home of one of the leading Pharisees; and people were watching Jesus closely. A man whose legs and arms were swollen came to Jesus, and Jesus spoke up and asked the teachers of the Law and the Pharisees, "Does our Law allow healing on the Sabbath, or not?"

But they would not say a thing. Jesus took the man, healed him and sent him away. Then he said to them, "If any one of you had a son or an ox that happened to fall in a well on a Sabbath, would you not pull him out at once on the Sabbath itself?"

But they were not able to answer him about this.

### Humility and Hospitality

Jesus noticed how some of the guests were choosing the best places, so he told this parable to all of them, "When someone invites you to a wedding feast, do not sit down in the best place. It could happen that someone more important than you had been invited, and your host, who invited both of you, would come and say to you, 'Let him have this place.' Then you would be embarrassed and have to sit in the lowest place. Instead, when you are invited, go and sit in the lowest place, so that your host will come to you and say, 'Come on up, my friend, to a better place.' This will bring you honor in the presence of all the other guests. Because everyone who makes himself great will be humbled, and everyone who humbles himself will be made great."

Then Jesus said to his host, "When you give a lunch or a dinner, do not invite your friends or your brothers or your relatives or your rich neighbors — for they will invite you back, and in this way you will be paid for what you did. When you give a feast, invite the poor, the crippled, the lame, and the blind, and you will be blessed, because they are not able to pay you back. God will repay you on the day the good people rise from death."

### Jesus Visits Martha and Mary

As Jesus and his disciples went on their way, he came to a village where a woman named Martha welcomed him in her home. She had a sister named Mary, who sat down at the feet of the Lord and listened to his teaching. Martha was upset over all the work she had to do; so she came and said, "Lord, don't you care that my sister has left me to do all the work by myself? Tell her to come and help me!"

The Lord answered her, "Martha, Martha! You are worried and troubled over so many things, but just one is needed. Mary has chosen the right thing, and it will not be taken away from her."

### The Request of James and John

Then James and John, the sons of Zebedee, came to Jesus. "Teacher," they said, "there is something we want you to do for us."

"What is it?" Jesus asked them.

They answered, "When you sit on your throne in your glorious Kingdom, we want you to let us sit with you, one at your right and one at your left."

Jesus said to them, "You don't know what you are asking for. Can

86

you drink the cup of suffering that I must drink? Can you be baptized in the way I must be baptized?"

"We can," they answered.

Jesus said to them, "You will indeed drink the cup I must drink and be baptized in the way I must be baptized. But I do not have the right to choose who will sit at my right and my left. It is God who will give these places to those for whom he has prepared them."

When the other ten disciples heard about it, they became angry with James and John. So Jesus called them all together to him and said, "You know that the men who are considered rulers of the heathen have power over them, and the leaders have complete authority. This, however, is not the way it is among you. If one of you wants to be great, he must be the servant of the rest; and if one of you wants to be first, he must be the slave of all. For even the Son of Man did not come to be served; he came to serve and to give his life to redeem many people."

*Jesus' Love for Jerusalem*

Some Pharisees came to Jesus and said to him. "You must get out of here and go somewhere else, because Herod wants to kill you."

Jesus answered them, "Go and tell that fox: 'I am driving out demons and performing cures today and tomorrow, and on the third day I shall finish my work.' Yet I must be on my way today, tomorrow, and the

next day; it is not right for a prophet to be killed anywhere except in Jerusalem.

"Jerusalem, Jerusalem! You kill the prophets, you stone the messengers God has sent you! How many times I wanted to put my arms round all your people, just as a hen gathers her chicks under her wings, but you would not let me! And so your Temple will be abandoned. I assure you that you will not see me until the time comes when you say, 'God bless him who comes in the name of the Lord.' "

## Jesus Enters Jerusalem

### Jesus Heals a Blind Beggar

As Jesus was coming near Jericho, there was a blind man sitting by the road, begging. When he heard the crowd passing by he asked, "What is this?"

"Jesus of Nazareth is passing by," they told him.

He cried out, "Jesus! Son of David! Have mercy on me!"

The people in front scolded him and told him to be quiet. But he shouted even more loudly, "Son of David! Have mercy on me!"

So Jesus stopped and ordered that the blind man be brought to him. When he came near, Jesus asked him, "What do you want me to do for you?"

"Sir," he answered, "I want to see again."

Then Jesus said to him, "Then see! Your faith has made you well."

At once he was able to see, and he followed Jesus, giving thanks to God. When the crowd saw it, they all praised God.

### Jesus and Zacchaeus

Jesus went on into Jericho and was passing through. There was a chief tax collector there named Zacchaeus, who was rich. He was trying to see who Jesus was, but he was a little man and could not see Jesus because of the crowd. So he ran ahead of the crowd and climbed a sycamore tree to see Jesus, who was going that way. When Jesus came to that place he looked up and said to Zacchaeus, "Hurry down, Zacchaeus, because I must stay in your house today."

Zacchaeus hurried down and welcomed him with great joy. All the people who saw it started grumbling, "This man has gone as a guest to the home of a sinner!"

Zacchaeus stood up and said to the Lord, "Listen, sir! I will give half my belongings to the poor, and if I have cheated anyone, I will pay him back four times as much."

Jesus said to him, "Salvation has come to this house today for this man, also, is a descendant of Abraham. For the Son of Man came to seek and to save the lost."

## The Triumphant Entry into Jerusalem

As they approached Jerusalem, near the towns of Bethphage and Bethany they came to the Mount of Olives. Jesus sent two of his disciples on ahead with these instructions: "Go to the village there ahead of you. As soon as you get there, you will find a colt tied up that has never been ridden. Untie it and bring it here. And if someone asks you why you are doing that, tell him that the Master needs it and will send it back at once."

So they went and found a colt out in the street, tied to the door of a house. As they were untying it, some of the bystanders asked them, "What are you doing untying that colt?"

They answered just as Jesus had told them, and the men let them go. They brought the colt to Jesus, threw their cloaks over the animal, and Jesus got on. Many people spread their cloaks on the road, while others

cut branches in the field and spread them on the road. The people who were in front and those who followed behind began to shout, "Praise God! God bless him who comes in the name of the Lord! God bless the coming kingdom of King David, our father! Praise be to God!"

Jesus entered Jerusalem, went into the Temple, and looked round at everything. But since it was already late in the day, he went out to Bethany with the twelve disciples.

*Jesus Goes to the Temple*

When they arrived in Jerusalem, Jesus went to the Temple and began to drive out all those who were buying and selling. He overturned the tables of the moneychangers and the stools of those who sold pigeons, and would not let anyone carry anything through the temple courtyards. He then taught the people: "It is written in the Scriptures that God said, 'My Temple will be called a house of prayer for the people of all nations.' But you have turned it into a hideout for thieves!" The chief priest and the teachers of the Law heard of this, so they began looking for some way to kill Jesus. They were afraid of him, because the whole crowd was amazed at his teaching. When evening came, Jesus and his disciples left the city.

### The Question about Jesus' Authority

They arrived once again in Jerusalem. As Jesus was walking in the Temple, the chief priests, the teachers of the Law, and the elders came to him and asked him, "What right do you have to do these things? Who gave you such right?"

Jesus answered them, "I will ask you just one question, and if you give me an answer, I will tell you what right I have to do these things. Tell me, where did John's right to baptize come from: was it from God or from men?"

They started to argue among themselves: "What shall we say? If we answer, 'From God,' he will say, 'Why, then, did you not believe John?' But if we say, 'From man . . .'" (They were afraid of the people, because everyone was convinced that John had been a prophet.) So their answer to Jesus was, "We don't know."

Jesus said to them, "Neither will I tell you, then, by what right I do these things."

### The Widow's Offering

As Jesus sat near the temple treasury he watched the people as they dropped in their money. Many rich men dropped in much money; then a poor widow came along and dropped in two little copper coins, worth about a penny. He called his disciples together and said to them, "I tell you that this poor widow put more in the offering box than all the others. For the others put in what they had to spare of their riches; but she, poor as she is, put in all she had — she gave all she had to live on."

### Jesus Speaks of the Destruction of the Temple

As Jesus was leaving the Temple, one of his disciples said, "Look, Teacher! What wonderful stones and buildings!"

Jesus answered, "You see these great buildings? Not a single stone here will be left in its place; everyone of them will be thrown down."

### Troubles and Persecutions

Jesus was sitting on the Mount of Olives, across from the Temple, when

Peter, James, John, and Andrew came to him in private. "Tell us when this will be," they said, "and tell us what will happen to show that the time has come for all these things to take place."

Jesus said to them, "Watch out, and don't let anyone fool you. 'Many men, claiming to speak for me, will come and say, 'I am he!' and they will fool many people. And don't be troubled when you hear the noise of battles close by and news of battles far away. Such things must happen, but they do not mean that the end has come. Countries will fight each other, kingdoms will attack one another. There will be earthquakes everywhere, and there will be famines. These things are like the first pains of childbirth.

You yourselves must watch out. You will be arrested and taken to court. You will be beaten in the synagogues; you will stand before rulers and kings for my sake to tell them the Good News. But before the end comes, the gospel must be preached to all peoples. And when you are arrested and taken to court, do not worry ahead of time about what you are going to say; when the time comes, say whatever is then given to you. For the words you speak will not be yours; they will come from the Holy Spirit. Men will hand over their own brothers to be put to death, and fathers will do the same to their children. Children will turn against their parents and have them put to death. Everyone will hate you because of me. But whoever holds out to the end will be saved."

# 6
# How Jesus Died

*Jesus died as he lived. He was the humble servant of God, the loving brother of everyone. The story tells of how he was betrayed and left alone, how he was condemned to torture and death, and how he died full of courage and love. He gave his spirit back to God his Father, after this perfect sacrifice of his own life.*

*Many millions of people have been grateful for this, and their lives have been changed by this story. It is given here in the words of Mark, although at the end a few sentences are added from John and Luke.*

### The Plot against Jesus

It was now two days before the Festival of Passover and Unleavened Bread. The chief priests and the teachers of the Law were looking for a way to arrest Jesus secretly and put him to death. "We must not do it during the festival," they said, "or the people might riot."

### Jesus Anointed at Bethany

Jesus was in Bethany at the house of Simon, a man who had suffered from a dreaded skin disease. While Jesus was eating a woman came in with an alabaster jar full of a very expensive perfume made of pure nard. She broke the jar and poured the perfume on Jesus' head. Some of the people there became angry, and said to one another, "What was the use of wasting the perfume? It could have been sold for more than three hundred silver coins, and the money given to the poor!" And they criticized her harshly.

But Jesus said, "Leave her alone! Why are you bothering her? She has done a fine and beautiful thing for me. You will always have poor people with you, and any time you want to, you can help them. But you shall not always have me. She did what she could; she poured perfume on my body to prepare it ahead of time for burial. Now, I assure you that wherever the gospel is preached all over the world, what she has done will be told in memory of her."

### Judas Agrees to Betray Jesus

Then Judas Iscariot, one of the twelve disciples, went off to the chief priests in order to betray Jesus to them. They were greatly pleased to hear what he had to say, and promised to give him money. So Judas started looking for a good chance to hand Jesus over to them.

### Jesus Eats the Passover Meal with his Disciples

On the first day of the Festival of Unleavened Bread, the day the lambs for the Passover meal were killed, Jesus' disciples asked him, "Where do you want us to go and get the Passover meal ready for you?"

Then Jesus sent two of them out with these instructions: "Go into the city, and a man carrying a jar of water will meet you. Follow him to the house he enters, and say to the owner of the house: 'The Teacher says, Where is my room where my disciples and I will eat the Passover meal?' Then he will show you a large upstairs room, fixed up and furnished, where you will get everything ready for us."

The disciples left, went to the city, and found everything just as Jesus had told them; and they prepared the Passover meal.

When it was evening, Jesus came with the twelve disciples. While they were at the table eating, Jesus said, "I tell you that one of you will betray me — one who is eating with me."

The disciples were upset and began to ask him, one after the other, "Surely you don't mean me, do you?"

Jesus answered, "It will be one of you twelve, one who dips his bread in the dish with me. The Son of Man will die as the Scriptures say he will; but how terrible for that man who will betray the Son of Man! It would have been better for that man if he had never been born!"

### The Lord's Supper

While they were eating, Jesus took a piece of bread, gave a prayer of thanks, broke it, and gave it to his disciples. "Take it," he said, "this is my body."

Then he took a cup, gave thanks to God, and handed it to them; and they all drank from it. Jesus said, "This is my blood which is poured out for many, my blood which seals God's covenant. I tell you, I will never again drink this wine until the day I drink the new wine in the Kingdom of God."

Then they sang a hymn and went out to the Mount of Olives.

### Jesus Predicts Peter's Denial

Jesus said to them, "All of you will run away and leave me, for the the scripture says, 'God will kill the shepherd and the sheep will all be scattered.' But after I am raised to life I will go to Galilee ahead of you."

Peter answered, "I will never leave you, even though all the rest do!"

Jesus said to Peter. "I tell you that before the rooster crows two times tonight, you will say three times that you do not know me."

Peter answered even more strongly, "I will never say that, even if I have to die with you!"

And all the disciples said the same thing.

### Jesus Prays in Gethsemane

They came to a place called Gethsemane, and Jesus said to his disciples, "Sit here while I pray."

He took Peter, James, and John with him. Distress and anguish came over him, and he said to them, "The sorrow in my heart is so great that it almost crushes me. Stay here and keep watch."

He went a little farther on, threw himself on the ground and prayed that, if possible, he might not have to go through that time of suffering. "Father!" he prayed, "my Father! All things are possible for you. Take this cup of suffering away from me. Yet not what I want, but what you want."

Then he returned and found the three disciples asleep. He said to Peter, "Simon, are you asleep? Weren't you able to stay awake for even one hour?" And he said to them, "Keep watch, and pray that you will not fall into temptation. The spirit is willing, but the flesh is weak."

He went away once more and prayed, saying the same words. Then he came back to the disciples and found them asleep; they could not keep their eyes open. And they did not know what to say to him.

When he came back the third time, he said to them, "Are you still sleeping and resting? Enough! The hour has come! Look, the Son of Man is now handed over to the power of sinful men. Get up, let us go. Look, here is the man who is betraying me!"

### The Arrest of Jesus

Jesus was still speaking when Judas, one of the twelve disciples, arrived. With him was a crowd armed with swords and clubs and sent by the chief priests, the teachers of the Law, and the elders. The traitor had given the crowd a signal: "The man I kiss is the one you want. Arrest him and take him away under guard."

As soon as Judas arrived he went up to Jesus and said, "Teacher!" and kissed him. So they arrested Jesus and held him tight. But one of those standing there drew his sword and struck at the High Priest's slave, cutting off his ear. Then Jesus spoke up and said to them. "Did you have to come with swords and clubs to capture me, as though I were an outlaw? Day after day I was with you teaching in the Temple, and you did not arrest me. But the Scriptures must come true."

Then all the disciples left him and ran away.

A certain young man, dressed only in a linen cloth, was following Jesus. They tried to arrest him, but he ran away naked, leaving the cloth behind.

*Jesus before the Council*

Then Jesus was taken to the High Priest's house, where all the chief priests, the elders, and the teachers of the Law were gathering. Peter followed from a distance and went into the courtyard of the High Priest's house. There he sat down with the guards, keeping himself warm by the fire. The chief priests and the whole Council tried to find some evidence against Jesus in order to put him to death, but they could not find any. Many witnesses told lies against Jesus, but their stories did not agree.

Then some men stood up and told this lie against Jesus, "We heard him say, 'I will tear down this Temple which men made, and after three days I will build one that is not made by men.'" Not even they, however, could make their stories agree.

The High Priest stood up in front of them all and questioned Jesus, "Have you no answer to the accusation they bring against you?"

But Jesus kept quiet and would not say a word. Again the High Priest questioned him, "Are you the Messiah, the Son of the Blessed God?"

"I am," answered Jesus, "and you will all see the Son of Man seated at the right side of the Almighty, and coming with the clouds of Heaven!"

The High Priest tore his robes and said, "We don't need any more witnesses! You heard his blasphemy. What is your decision?"

They all voted against him: he was guilty and should be put to death.

Some of them began to spit on Jesus, and they blindfolded him and hit him. "Guess who hit you!" they said. And the guards took him and slapped him.

*Peter Denies Jesus*

Peter was still down in the courtyard when one of the High Priest's servant girls came by. When she saw Peter warming himself, she looked straight at him and said, "You, too, were with Jesus of Nazareth."

But he denied it. "I don't know . . . I don't understand what you are talking about," he answered, and went into the passageway; just then a rooster crowed.

The servant girl saw him there and began to repeat to the bystanders, "He is one of them!" But Peter denied it again.

A little while later the bystanders accused Peter again, "You can't deny that you are one of them, because you, too, are from Galilee."

Then Peter said; "I swear that I am telling the truth! May God punish me if I am not! I do not know the man you are talking about!"

Just then a rooster crowed a second time, and Peter remembered how Jesus had said to him, "Before the rooster crows two times, you will say three times that you do not know me." And he broke down and cried.

## Jesus before Pilate

Early in the morning the chief priests met hurriedly with the elders, the teachers of the Law, and the whole Council, and made their plans. They put Jesus in chains, led him away and handed him over to Pilate. Pilate questioned him, "Are you the king of the Jews?"

Jesus answered, "So you say."

The chief priests were accusing Jesus of many things, so Pilate questioned him again, "Aren't you going to answer? Listen to all their accusations!"

Again Jesus refused to say a word, and Pilate was amazed.

## Jesus is Sentenced to Death

At every Passover Festival Pilate was in the habit of setting free any one prisoner the people asked for. At that time a man named Barabbas was in prison with the rebels who had committed murder in the riot. When the crowd gathered and began to ask Pilate for the usual favor, he asked them, "Do you want me to set free for you the king of the Jews?" He knew very well that the chief priests had handed Jesus over to him because they were jealous.

But the chief priests stirred up the crowd to ask, instead, that Pilate set Barabbas free for them. Pilate spoke again to the crowd, "What, then, do you want me to do with the one you call the king of the Jews?"

They shouted back, "Crucify him!"

"But what crime has he committed?" Pilate asked.

They shouted all the louder, "Crucify him!"

Pilate wanted to please the crowd, so he set Barabbas free for them. Then he had Jesus whipped and handed over to be crucified.

## The Soldiers Make Fun of Jesus

The soldiers took Jesus inside the courtyard of the governor's palace and called together the rest of the company. They put a purple robe on Jesus, made a crown out of thorny branches, and put it on his head. Then they began to salute him: "Long live the King of the Jews!" They beat him over the head with a stick, spat on him, fell on their knees and bowed down to him. When they had finished making fun of him, they took off the purple robe and put his own clothes back on him. Then they led him out to crucify him.

## Jesus is Crucified

On the way they met a man named Simon, who was coming into the city from the country, and the soldiers forced him to carry Jesus' cross.

(Simon was from Cyrene and was the father of Alexander and Rufus.) They took Jesus to a place called Golgotha, which means "The Place of the Skull". There they tried to give him wine mixed with a drug called myrrh, but Jesus would not drink it. Then they crucified him and divided his clothes among themselves, throwing dice to see who would get which piece of clothing. It was nine o'clock in the morning when they crucified him. The notice of the accusation against him said: "The King of Jews". They also crucified two bandits with Jesus, one on his right and the other on his left. (In this way the scripture came true which says, "He shared the fate of criminals.")

Jesus said, "Forgive them, Father! They don't know what they are doing."

People passing by shook their heads and hurled insults at Jesus: "Aha! You were going to tear down the Temple and build it back up in three days! Now come down from the cross and save yourself!"

In the same way the chief priests and the teachers of the Law made fun of Jesus, saying to one another, "He saved others, but he cannot save himself! Let us see the Messiah, the king of Israel, come down from the cross now, and we will believe in him!"

One of the criminals hanging there hurled insults at him, "Aren't you the Messiah? Save yourself and us!"

The other one, however, rebuked him, saying, "Don't you fear God? You received the same sentence he did. Ours, however, is only right, because we are getting what we deserve for what we did; but he has done no wrong." And he said to Jesus, "Remember me, Jesus, when you come as King!"

Jesus said to him, "I tell you that: today you will be in Paradise with me."

Standing close to Jesus' cross were his mother, his mother's sister, Mary the wife of Clopas, and Mary Magdalene. Jesus saw his mother and the disciple he loved standing there; so he said to his mother, "He is your son."

Then he said to the disciple, "She is your mother." From that time the disciple took her to live in his home.

## The Death of Jesus

At noon the whole country was covered with darkness, which lasted for three hours. At three o'clock Jesus cried out with a loud shout, *"Eloi, Eloi, lema sabachthani?"* which means, "My God, my God, why did you abandon me?"

Some of the people there heard him and said, "Listen, he is calling for Elijah!" One of them ran up with a sponge, soaked it in cheap wine, and put it on the end of a stick. Then he held it up to Jesus' lips and

said, "Wait! Let us see if Elijah is coming to bring him down from the cross!"

Jesus knew that by now everything had been completed; and in order to make the scripture come true he said, "I am thirsty."

A bowl was there, full of cheap wine; so a sponge was soaked in the wine, put on a stalk of hyssop, and lifted up to his lips. Jesus drank the wine and said, "It is finished!"

Jesus cried out in a loud voice, "Father! In your hands I place my spirit!" He said this and died.

The army officer saw what had happened, and he praised God, saying, "Certainly he was a good man!"

When the people who had gathered there to watch the spectacle saw what happened, they all went back home, beating their breasts in sorrow. All those who knew Jesus personally, including the women who had followed him from Galilee, stood off at a distance to watch.

## The Burial of Jesus

There was a man named Joseph from Arimathea, a town in Judea. He was a good and honorable man, who was waiting for the coming of the Kingdom of God. Although a member of the Council, he had not agreed with their decision and action. He went into the presence of Pilate and asked for the body of Jesus. Then he took the body down, wrapped it in a linen sheet, and placed it in a tomb which had been dug out of solid rock and which had never been used. It was Friday, and the Sabbath was about to begin.

The women who had followed Jesus from Galilee went with Joseph and saw the tomb and how Jesus' body was placed in it. Then they went back home and prepared the spices and ointments for the body.

On the Sabbath they rested, as the Law commanded.

# 7
# The Victory of Jesus

*The death of Jesus was not the end. His followers saw him alive, and knew Him as Lord and Savior. We today can read some of the stories they told about His resurrection. Here, extracts are given from three gospels — by John, Luke and Matthew — giving glimpses of the first Christians and their living Lord. And as we read, we can join in the prayer of the doubter, Thomas, to Jesus: "My Lord and my God!" This certainty that Jesus was Lord did not grow less when the first Easter had passed. The stories of Stephen and of Saul (who became Saint Paul) show how people still saw Jesus in his glory and his power. The Revelation written by John "the Divine" is the record of another vision of King Jesus.*

## The Empty Tomb

Early on Sunday morning, while it was still dark, Mary Magdalene went to the tomb and saw that the stone had been taken away from the entrance: She went running to Simon Peter and the other disciple, whom Jesus loved, and told them, "They have taken the Lord from the tomb and we don't know where they have put him!"

Then Peter and the other disciple went to the tomb. The two of them were running, but the other disciple ran faster than Peter and reached the tomb first. He bent over and saw the linen cloths, but he did not go in. Behind him came Simon Peter, and he went straight into the tomb. He saw the linen cloths lying there and the cloth which had been round Jesus' head. It was not lying with the linen cloths but was rolled up by itself. Then the other disciple, who had reached the tomb first, also went in; he saw and believed. (They still did not understand the scripture which said that he must rise from death.) Then the disciples went back home.

## Jesus Appears to Mary Magdalene

Mary stood crying outside the tomb. While she was still crying, she bent over and looked in the tomb and saw two angels there dressed in white, sitting where the body of Jesus had been, one at the head and the other at the feet. "Woman, why are you crying?" they asked her.

She answered, "They have taken my Lord away, and I do not know where they have put him!"

Then she turned around and saw Jesus standing there; but she did not know that it was Jesus. "Woman, why are you crying?" Jesus asked her. "Who is it that you are looking for?"

She thought he was the gardener, so she said to him, "If you took him away, sir, tell me where you have put him, and I will go and get him."

Jesus said to her, "Mary!"

She turned towards him and said in Hebrew, "Rabboni!" (This means "Teacher".)

"Do not hold on to me," Jesus told her, "because I have not yet gone back up to the Father. But go to my brothers and tell them that I am returning to him who is my Father and their Father, my God and their God.'"

So Mary Magdalene went and told the disciples that she had seen the Lord and related to them what he had told her.

## The Walk to Emmaus

On that same day two of Jesus' followers were going to a village named Emmaus, about seven miles from Jerusalem, and they were talking to

each other about all the things that had happened. As they talked and discussed, Jesus himself drew near and walked along with them; they saw him, but somehow did not recognize him. Jesus said to them, "What are you talking about to each other, as you walk along?"

They stood still, with sad faces. One of them, named Cleopas, asked him, "Are you the only visitor in Jerusalem who doesn't know the things that have been happening there these last few days?"

"What things?" he asked.

"The things that happened to Jesus of Nazareth," they answered. "This man was a prophet, and was considered by God and by all the people to be powerful in everything he said and did. Our chief priests and rulers handed him over to be sentenced to death, and he was crucified. And we had hoped that he would be the one who was going to set Israel free! Besides all that, this is now the third day since it happened. Some of the women of our group surprised us; they went at dawn to the tomb, but could not find his body. They came back saying they had seen a vision of angels who told them that he is alive. Some of our group went to the tomb and found it exactly as the women had said, but they did not see him."

Then Jesus said to them, "How foolish you are, how slow you are to believe everything the prophets said! Was it not necessary for the Messiah to suffer these things and then to enter his glory?" And Jesus explained to them what was said about himself in all the Scriptures, beginning with the books of Moses and the writings of all the prophets.

As they came near the village to which they were going, Jesus acted as if he were going farther; but they held him back, saying, "Stay with us; the day is almost over and it is getting dark." So he went in to stay with them. He sat down to eat with them, took the bread, and said the blessing; then he broke the bread and gave it to them. Then their eyes were opened and they recognized him, but he disappeared from their sight. They said to each other, "Wasn't it like a fire burning in us when he talked to us on the road and explained the Scriptures to us?"

They got up at once and went back to Jerusalem, where they found the eleven disciples gathered together with the others and saying, "The Lord is risen indeed! He has appeared to Simon!"

The two then explained to them what had happened on the road, and how they had recognized the Lord when he broke the bread.

### Jesus Appears to his Disciples

It was late that Sunday evening, and the disciples were gathered together behind locked doors, because they were afraid of the Jewish authorities. Then Jesus came and stood among them. "Peace be with you," he said. After saying this he showed them his hands and his side.

114

The disciples were filled with joy at seeing the Lord. Jesus said to them again, "Peace be with you. As the Father sent me, so I send you," Then he breathed on them and said, "Receive the Holy Spirit. If you forgive men's sins, they are forgiven; if you do not forgive them, they are not forgiven."

## Jesus and Thomas

One of the twelve disciples, Thomas (called the Twin), was not with them when Jesus came. So the other disciples told him, "We have seen the Lord!"

Thomas said to them, "Unless I see the scars of the nails in his hands, and put my finger on those scars, and my hand in his side, I will not believe."

A week later the disciples were together again indoors, and Thomas was with them. The doors were locked, but Jesus came and stood among them and said, "Peace be with you." Then he said to Thomas, "Put your finger here, and look at my hands; then reach out your hand and put it in my side. Stop your doubting, and believe!"

Thomas answered him, "My Lord and my God!"

Jesus said to him, "Do you believe because you see me? How happy are those who believe without seeing me!"

## Jesus Appears to Seven Disciples

After this, Jesus appeared once more to his disciples at Lake Tiberias. This is how it happened. Simon Peter, Thomas (called the Twin), Nathanael (the one from Cana in Galilee), the sons of Zebedee, the two other disciples of Jesus were all together. Simon Peter said to the others, "I am going fishing."

"We will come with you," they told him. So they went out in a boat, but all that night they did not catch a thing. As the sun was rising, Jesus stood at the water's edge, but the disciples did not know that it was Jesus. Then he said to them, "Young men, haven't you caught anything?"

"Not a thing," they answered.

He said to them, "Throw your net out on the right side of the boat, and you will catch some." So they threw the net out and could not pull it back in, because they had caught so many fish.

The disciple whom Jesus loved said to Peter, "It is the Lord!" When Peter heard that it was the Lord, he wrapped his outer garment round him (for he had taken his clothes off) and jumped into the water. The other disciples came to shore in the boat, pulling the net full of fish. They were not very far from land, about a hundred yards away. When they stepped ashore they saw a charcoal fire there with fish on it and some bread. Then Jesus said to them, "Bring some of the fish you have just caught."

Simon Peter went aboard and dragged the net ashore, full of big fish, a hundred and fifty-three in all; even though there were so many, still the net did not tear. Jesus said to them, "Come and eat." None of the disciples dared ask him, "Who are you?" because they knew it was the Lord. So Jesus went over, took the bread, and gave it to them; he did the same with the fish.

This, then, was the third time Jesus showed himself to the disciples after he was raised from death.

## Jesus and Peter

After they had eaten, Jesus said to Simon Peter, "Simon son of John, do you love me more than these others do?"

"Yes, Lord," he answered, "you know that I love you."

Jesus said to him, "Take care of my lambs." A second time Jesus said to him, "Simon son of John, do you love me?"

"Yes, Lord," he answered, you know that I love you."

Jesus said to him, "Take care of my sheep." A third time Jesus said, "Simon son of John, do you love me?"

Peter became sad because Jesus asked him the third time, "Do you love me?" and so he said to him, "Lord, you know everything; you know I love you!"

Jesus said to him, "Take care of my sheep. I am telling you the truth: when you were young, you used to get ready and go anywhere you wanted to; but when you are old, you will stretch out your hands and someone else will tie you up and take you where you don't want to go." (In saying this, Jesus was indicating the way in which Peter would die and bring glory to God.) Then Jesus said to him, "Follow me!"

## Jesus and the Other Disciple

Peter turned around and saw behind him that other disciple, whom Jesus loved — the one who had leaned close to Jesus at the meal and asked, "Lord, who is going to betray you?" When Peter saw him, he asked Jesus, "Lord, what about this man?"

Jesus answered him, "If I want him to live until I come, what is that to you? Follow me!"

So a report spread among the followers of Jesus that this disciple would not die. But Jesus did not say he would not die; he said, "If I want him to live until I come, what is that to you?"

He is the disciple who spoke of these things, the one who also wrote them down; and we know that what he said is true.

*Jesus Appears to his Disciples*

The eleven disciples went to the hill in Galilee where Jesus had told them to go. When they saw him they worshiped him, even though some of them doubted. Jesus drew near and said to them, "I have been given all authority in heaven and on earth. Go, then, to all peoples everywhere and make them my disciples: baptize them in the name of the Father, the Son, and the Holy Spirit, and teach them to obey everything I have commanded you. And I will be with you always, to the end of the age."

## Stephen and Saul See Jesus in his Glory

*The Arrest of Stephen*

Stephen, a man richly blessed by God and full of power, performed great miracles and wonders among the people. But he was opposed by some men who were members of the synagogue of the Freedmen (as it was called), which had Jews from Cyrenia and Alexandria. They and other Jews from the provinces of Cilicia and Asia started arguing with Stephen. But the Spirit gave Stephen such wisdom that when he spoke, they could not refute him. So they bribed some men to say, "We heard him speaking against Moses and against God!" In this way they stirred up the people, the elders, and the teachers of the Law. They seized Stephen and took him before the Council. Then they brought in some men to tell lies about him. "This man," they said, "is always talking against our sacred Temple and the Law of Moses. We heard him say that this Jesus of Nazareth will tear down the Temple and change all the customs which have come down to us from Moses!" All those sitting in the Council fixed their eyes on Stephen and saw that his face looked like the face of an angel.

*The Stoning of Stephen*

As the members of the Council listened to Stephen they became furious and ground their teeth at him in anger. But Stephen, full of the Holy Spirit, looked up to heaven and saw God's glory and Jesus standing at the right side of God. "Look!" he said. "I see heaven opened and the Son of Man standing at the right side of God!"

With a loud cry the Council members covered their ears with their hands. Then they all rushed at him at once, threw him out of the city and stoned him. The witnesses left their cloaks in the care of a young man named Saul. They kept on stoning Stephen as he called out to the Lord, "Lord Jesus, receive my spirit!" He knelt down and cried in a loud voice, "Lord! Do not remember this sin against them!" He said this and died.

And Saul approved of his murder.

## Saul Persecutes the Church

That very day the church in Jerusalem began to suffer cruel persecution. All the believers, except the apostles, were scattered throughout the provinces of Judea and Samaria. Some devout men buried Stephen, mourning for him with loud cries.

But Saul tried to destroy the church; going from house to house, he dragged out the believers, both men and women, and threw them into jail.

## The Conversion of Saul

Saul kept up his violent threats of murder against the followers of the Lord. He went to the High Priest and asked for letters of introduction to the synagogues in Damascus, so that if he should find any followers of the Way of the Lord there, he would be able to arrest them, both men and women, and bring them back to Jerusalem.

As Saul was coming near the city of Damascus, suddenly a light from the sky flashed round him. He fell to the ground and heard a voice saying to him, "Saul, Saul! Why do you persecute me?"

"Who are you, Lord?" he asked.

"I am Jesus, whom you persecute," the voice said. "But get up and go into the city, where you will be told what you must do."

The men who were traveling with Saul had stopped, not saying a word; they heard the voice but could not see anyone. Saul got up from the ground and opened his eyes, but could not see a thing. So they took him by the hand and led him into Damascus. For three days he was not able to see, and during that time he did not eat or drink anything.

There was a Christian in Damascus named Ananias. He had a vision, in which the Lord said to him, "Ananias!"

"Here I am, Lord," he answered.

The Lord said to him, "Get ready and go to Straight Street, and at the house of Judas ask for a man from Tarsus named Saul. He is praying and in a vision he has seen a man named Ananias come in and place his hands on him so that he might see again."

Ananias answered, "Lord, many people have told me about this man, and about all the terrible things he has done to your people in Jerusalem. And he has come to Damascus with authority from the chief priests to arrest all who worship you."

The Lord said to him, "Go, because I have chosen him to serve me, to make my name known to Gentiles and kings and to the people of Israel. And I myself will show him all that he must suffer for my sake."

So Ananias went, entered the house where Saul was and placed his hands on him. "Brother Saul," he said, "the Lord has sent me — Jesus himself, who appeared to you on the road as you were coming here.

120

He sent me so that you might see again and be filled with the Holy Spirit." At once something like fish scales fell from Saul's eyes and he was able to see again. He stood up and was baptized; and after he had eaten, his strength came back.

### Saul Preaches in Damascus

Saul stayed for a few days with the believers in Damascus. He went straight to the synagogues and began to preach that Jesus, was the Son of God.

All who heard him were amazed, and asked, "Isn't he the one who in Jerusalem was killing those who worship that man Jesus? And didn't he come here for the very purpose of arresting those people and taking them back to the chief priests?"

## The Victory through our Lord Jesus Christ

*Paul, previously Saul the enemy of the Church, writes to the Corinthians*

### The Resurrection of Christ

And now I want to remind you, my brothers, of the Good News which I preached to you, which you received, and on which your faith stands firm. That is the gospel, the message that I preached to you. You are saved by the gospel if you hold firmly to it — unless it was for nothing that you believed.

I passed on to you what I received, which is of the greatest importance: that Christ died for our sins, as written in the Scriptures; that he was buried, and that he was raised to life three days later, as written in the Scriptures; that he appeared to Peter, and then to all twelve apostles. Then he appeared to more than five hundred of his followers at once, most of whom are still alive, although some have died. Then he appeared to James, and afterward to all the apostles.

Last of all he appeared also to me — even though I am like someone whose birth was abnormal. For I am the least of all the apostles — I do not even deserve to be called an apostle, because I persecuted God's church. But by God's grace I am what I am, and the grace that he gave me was not without effect. On the contrary, I have worked harder than any of the other apostles, although it was not really my own doing, but God's grace working with me. So then, whether it came from me or from them, this is what we all preach, this is what you believe.

### The Resurrection Body

Someone will ask, "How can the dead be raised to life? What kind of body will they have?" You fool! When you plant a seed in the ground, it does not sprout to life unless it dies. And what you plant is a bare seed, perhaps a grain of wheat or of some other grain, not the full-bodied plant that will later grow up. God provides that seed with the body he wishes; he gives each seed its own proper body.

And the flesh of living beings is not all the same kind of flesh; human beings have one kind of flesh, animals another, birds another, and fish another.

And there are heavenly bodies and earthly bodies; the beauty that belongs to heavenly bodies is different from the beauty that belongs to earthly bodies. The sun has its own beauty, the moon another beauty, and the stars a different beauty; and even among stars there are different kinds of beauty.

This is how it will be when the dead are raised to life. When the body is buried it is mortal, when raised, it will be immortal. When buried, it is ugly and weak; when raised, it will be beautiful and strong. When buried, it is a physical body; when raised, it will be a spiritual body. There is, of course, a physical body, so there has to be a spiritual body. For the scripture says, "The first man, Adam, was created a living being"; but the last Adam is the life-giving Spirit. It is not the spiritual that comes first, but the physical, and then the spiritual. The first Adam, made of earth, came from the earth; the second Adam came from heaven. Those who belong to the earth are like the one who was made of earth; those who are of heaven are like the one who came from heaven. Just as we wear the likeness of the man made of earth, so we will wear the likeness of the Man from heaven.

What I mean, brothers, is that: what is made of flesh and blood cannot share in God's Kingdom, and what is mortal cannot possess immortality.

Listen to this secret truth: we shall not all die, but when the last trumpet sounds, we shall all be changed in an instant as quickly as the blinking of an eye. For when the trumpet sounds, the dead will be raised, never to die again, and we shall all be changed. For what is mortal must be changed into what is immortal; what will die must be changed into what cannot die. So when this takes place, and the mortal has been changed into the immortal, then the Scripture will come true: "Death is destroyed; victory is complete!"

"Where, Death, is your victory?

Where, Death is your power to hurt?"

Death gets its power to hurt from sin, and sin gets its power from the Law. But thanks be to God who gives us the victory through our Lord Jesus Christ!

So then, my dear brothers, stand firm and steady. Keep busy always in your work for the Lord, since you know that nothing you do in the Lord's service is ever useless.

## The New Life is Stronger than Death

*Paul writes to the Romans*

### Life in the Spirit

There is no condemnation now for those who live in union with Christ Jesus. For the law of the Spirit, which brings us life in union with Christ Jesus, has set me free from the law of sin and death. What the Law could not do, because human nature was weak, God did. He condemned sin in human nature by sending his own Son, who came with a nature like man's sinful nature to do away with sin. God did this so that the righteous demands of the Law might be fully satisfied in us who live according to the Spirit, not according to human nature. Those who live as their human nature tells them to, have their minds controlled by what human nature wants. Those who live as the Spirit tells them to, have their minds controlled by what the Spirit wants. To be controlled by human nature results in death; to be controlled by the Spirit results in life and peace. And so a person becomes an enemy of God when he is controlled by human nature: for he does not obey God's law, and in fact he cannot obey it. Those who obey their human nature cannot please God.

But you do not live as your human nature tells you to; instead you live as the Spirit tells you to — if, in fact, God's Spirit lives in you. Whoever does not have the Spirit of Christ does not belong to him. But if Christ lives in you, the Spirit is life for you because you have been put right with God, even though your bodies are going to die because of sin. If the Spirit of God, who raised Jesus from death, lives in you, then he who raised Christ from death will also give life to your mortal bodies by the presence of his Spirit in you.

So then, my brothers, we have an obligation, but it is not to live as our human nature wants us to. For if you live according to your human nature, you are going to die; but if by the Spirit you put to death your sinful actions, you will live. Those who are led by God's Spirit are God's sons. For the Spirit that God has given you does not make you slaves and cause you to be afraid; instead, the Spirit makes you God's children, and by the Spirit's power we cry to God, "Father! my Father!" God's Spirit joins himself to our spirits to declare that we are God's children. Since we are his children, we will possess the blessings he keeps for his people, and we will also possess with Christ what God has kept for him; for if we share Christ's suffering, we will also share his glory.

### The Future Glory

I consider that what we suffer at this present time cannot be compared at all with the glory that is going to be revealed to us. All of creation waits with eager longing for God to reveal his sons. For creation was condemned to lose its purpose, not of its own will, but because God willed it to be so. Yet there was the hope that creation itself would one day be set free from its slavery to decay and would share the glorious freedom of the children of God. For we know that up to the present time all of creation groans with pain, like the pain of childbirth. But not just creation alone which groans; we who have the Spirit as the first of God's gifts also groan within ourselves as we wait for God to make us his sons and set our whole being free. For it was by hope that we were saved; but if we see what we hope for, then it is not really hope. For who hopes for something he sees? But if we hope for what we do not see, we wait for it with patience.

In the same way the Spirit also comes to help us, weak as we are. For we do not know how we ought to pray; the Spirit himself pleads with God for us in groans that words cannot express. And God, who sees into our hearts, knows what the thought of the Spirit is; because the Spirit pleads with God on behalf of his people and in accordance with his will.

We know that in all things God works for good with those who love him, those whom he has called according to his purpose. Those whom God had already chosen he also set apart to become like his Son, so that the Son would be the first among many brothers. And so those whom God set apart, he called; and those he called, he put right with himself, and he shared his glory with them.

## God's Love in Christ Jesus

In view of all this, what can we say? If God is for us, who can be against us? Certainly not God, who did not even keep back his own Son, but offered him for us all! He gave us his Son — will he not also freely give us all things? Who will accuse God's chosen people? God himself declares them not guilty! Who, then, will condemn them? Not Christ Jesus, who died, or rather, who was raised to life and is at the right side of God, pleading with him for us! Who then, can separate us from the love of Christ? Can trouble do it, or hardship or persecution or hunger or poverty or danger or death? As the Scripture says,

"For your sake we are in danger of death at all times;
we are treated like sheep that are going to be slaughtered."

No, in all these things we have complete victory through him who loved us! For I am certain that nothing can separate us from his love: neither death nor life, neither angels nor other heavenly rulers or powers, neither the present nor the future, neither the world above nor the world below — there is nothing in all creation that will ever be able to separate us from the love of God which is ours through Christ Jesus our Lord.

## Jesus is Lord

*John the Divine writes to Christians in Asia from the prison on the island of Patmos*

From John to the seven churches in the province of Asia:

Grace and peace be yours from God, who is, who was, and who is to come, and from the seven spirits in front of his throne, and from Jesus Christ, the faithful witness, the firstborn Son, who was raised from death and who is also the ruler of the kings of the world.

He loves us, and by his death he has freed us from our sins and made us a kingdom of priests to serve his God and Father. To Jesus Christ be the glory and power forever and ever! Amen.

Look, he is coming on the clouds! Everyone will see him, including those who pierced him. All peoples on earth will mourn over him. So shall it be!

"I am the first and the last," says the Lord God Almighty, who is, who was, and who is to come.

### A Vision of Christ

I am John, your brother, and as a follower of Jesus I am your partner in patiently enduring the suffering that comes to those who belong to his Kingdom. I was put on the island of Patmos because I had proclaimed God's word and the truth that Jesus revealed. On the Lord's day the Spirit took control of me, and I heard a loud voice, that sounded like a trumpet, speaking behind me. It said, "Write down what you see, and send the book to the churches in the seven cities: Ephesus, Smyrna, Pergamum, Thyatira, Sardis, Philadelphia, and Laodicea."

I turned around to see who was talking to me, and I saw seven gold lampstands, and among them there was what looked like a human being, wearing a robe that reached to his feet, and a gold band round his chest. His hair was white as wool, or as snow, and his eyes blazed like fire; his feet shone like brass that has been refined and polished, and his voice sounded like a roaring waterfall. He held seven stars in his right hand, and a sharp two-edged sword came out of his mouth. His face was as bright as the midday sun. When I saw him, I fell down at his feet like a dead man. He placed his right hand on me and said, "Don't be afraid! I am the first and the last. I am the living one! I was dead, but now I am alive forever and ever. I have authority over death and the world of the dead. Write, then, the things you see, both the things that are now, and the things that will happen afterwards. Here is the secret meaning of the seven stars that you see in my right hand, and of the seven gold lampstands: the seven stars are the angels of the seven churches, and the seven lampstands are the seven churches."

*The New Heaven and the New Earth*

Then I saw a new heaven and a new earth. The first heaven and the first earth disappeared, and the sea vanished. And I saw the Holy City, the new Jerusalem, coming down out of heaven from God, prepared and ready, like a bride dressed to meet her husband. I heard a loud voice speaking from the throne, "Now God's home is with mankind! He will live with them, and they shall be his people. God himself will be with them, and he will be their God. He will wipe away all tears from their eyes. There will be no more death, no more grief or crying or pain. The old things have disappeared."

Then the one who sits on the throne said, "And now I make all things new!" He also said to me, "Write this, because these words are true and can be trusted." And he said, "It is done! I am the first and the last, the beginning and the end. To anyone who is thirsty I will give the right to drink from the spring of the water of life without paying for it. Whoever wins the victory will receive this from me: I will be his God, and he will be my son. But cowards, traitors, perverts, murderers, the immoral, those who practice magic, those who worship idols, and all liars — the place for them is the lake burning with fire and sulphur, which is the second death."

*The New Jerusalem*

One of the seven angels who had the seven bowls full of the seven last plagues came to me and said, "Come, and I will show you the Bride, the wife of the Lamb." The Spirit took control of me, and the angel carried me to the top of a very high mountain. He showed me Jerusalem, the Holy City, coming down out of heaven from God and shining with the glory of God. The city shone like a precious stone, like a jasper, clear as crystal. It had a great, high wall with twelve gates and with twelve angels in charge of the gates. On the gates were written the names of the twelve tribes of the people of Israel. There were three gates on each side; three on the east, three on the south, three on the north, and three on the west. The city's wall was built on twelve foundation stones, on which were written the names of the twelve apostles of the Lamb.

I did not see a temple in the city, because its temple is the Lord God Almighty and the Lamb. The city has no need of the sun or the moon to shine on it, because the glory of God shines on it, and the Lamb is its lamp. The peoples of the world will walk by its light, and the kings of the earth will bring their wealth into it. The gates of the city will stand open all day; they will never be closed, because there will be no night there. The greatness and the wealth of the nations will be brought into the city. But nothing that is impure will enter the city, nor anyone who

does shameful things or tells lies. Only those whose names are written in the Lamb's book of the living will enter the city.

The angel also showed me the river of the water of life, sparkling like crystal, and coming from the throne of God and of the Lamb and flowing down the middle of the city's street. On each side of the river was the tree of life, which bears fruit twelve times a year, once each month; and its leaves are for the healing of the nations.

The throne of God and of the Lamb will be in the city, and his servants will worship him. They will see his face, and his name will be written on their foreheads. There shall be no more night, and they will not need lamps or sunlight, because the Lord God will be their light, and they will rule as kings forever and ever.

## Two Early Christian Hymns

*quoted by Paul to the Philippians*

He always had the very nature of God,
    but he did not think that by force he should try to become
      equal with God.
Instead of this of his own free will he gave all he had,
    and took the nature of a servant.
He became like man,
    and appeared in human likeness.
He was humble and walked the path of obedience all the way
    to death — his death on the cross.
For this reason God raised him to the highest place above,
    and gave him the name that is greater than any other name.
And so, in honor of the name of Jesus
    all beings in heaven, on earth, and in the world below
    will fall on their knees,
and all will openly proclaim that Jesus Christ is Lord,
    to the glory of God the Father.

*and to Timothy*

If we have died with him,
    we shall also live with him.
If we continue to endure,
    we shall also rule with him.
If we deny him,
    he also will deny us.
If we are not faithful,
    he remains faithful,
    because he cannot be false to himself.

# 8
# We Saw his Glory

*The fourth gospel was written by John. It includes some facts about Jesus which are not given to us in the other three gospels, but its main purpose is to explain the meaning of Jesus' life. John was a very wise and holy man who saw deeply into this meaning.*

*We learn from this gospel that the life of Jesus is God's Word: "the Word became a human being and lived among us." The life of Jesus brings new joy, a new birth, a new knowledge of God. The life of Jesus is like bread to feed us, and it is like light to make us see; for Jesus is like a shepherd guiding us, and like a servant washing us.*

*When in John's gospel Jesus speaks to his friends at his last supper, and when he prays for them before his death, we are allowed to see the glory which John saw. It is the glory of perfect love.*

## The Light Shines

*The Word of Life*

Before the world was created, the Word already existed; he was with God, and he was the same as God. From the very beginning the Word was with God. Through him God made all things; not one thing in all creation was made without him. The Word was the source of life, and this life brought light to mankind. The light shines in the darkness, and the darkness has never put it out.

God sent his messenger, a man named John, who came to tell people about the light, so that all should hear the message and believe. He himself was not the light; he came to tell about the light. This was the real light — the light that comes into the world and shines on all mankind.

The Word then was in the world, and though God made the world through him, yet the world did not recognize him. He came to his own country, but his own people did not receive him. Some, however, did receive him and believed in him; so he gave them the right to become God's children. They did not become God's children by natural means, that is, by being born as the children of a human father; God himself was their Father.

The Word became a human being and, full of grace and truth, lived among us. We saw his glory, the glory which he received as the Father's only Son.

John spoke about him. He cried out, "This is the one I was talking about when I said, 'He comes after me, but he is greater than I am, because he existed before I was born.'"

Out of the fullness of his grace he has blessed us all, giving us one blessing after another. God gave the Law through Moses, but grace and truth came through Jesus Christ. No one has ever seen God. The only Son, who is the same as God and is at the Father's side, he has made him known.

## The Wedding at Cana

There was a wedding in the town of Cana in Galilee. Jesus' mother was there, and Jesus and his disciples had also been invited to the wedding. When the wine had given out, Jesus' mother said to him, "They are out of wine."

"You must not tell me what to do," Jesus replied. "My time has not yet come."

Jesus' mother then told the servants, "Do whatever he tells you."

The Jews have rules about ritual washing, and for this purpose six stone water jars were there, each one large enough to hold between twenty and thirty gallons. Jesus said to the servants, "Fill these jars with water." They filled them to the brim, and then he told them. "Now draw some water out and take it to the man in charge of the feast." They took him the water, which had turned into wine and he tasted it. He did not know where this wine had come from (but of course the servants who had drawn out the water knew); so he called the bridegroom and said to him, "Everyone else serves the best wine first, and after the guests have drunk a lot, he serves the ordinary wine. But you have kept the best wine until now!"

Jesus performed this first miracle in Cana of Galilee; there he revealed his glory, and his disciples believed in him.

## You Must All Be Born Again

*Jesus and Nicodemus*

There was a Jewish leader named Nicodemus, who belonged to the party of the Pharisees. One night he went to Jesus and said to him, "Rabbi, we know that you are a teacher sent by God. No one could perform the miracles you are doing unless God were with him."

Jesus answered, "I am telling you the truth: no one can see the Kingdom of God unless he is born again."

"How can a grown man be born again?" Nicodemus asked. "He certainly cannot enter his mother's womb and be born a second time!"

"I am telling you the truth," replied Jesus, "that no one can enter the Kingdom of God unless he is born of water and the Spirit. A person is born physically of human parents, but he is born spiritually of the Spirit. Do not be surprised because I tell you, that you must all be born again. The wind blows wherever it wishes; you hear the sound it makes, but you do not know where it comes from or where it is going. It is like that with everyone who is born of the Spirit."

"How can this be?" asked Nicodemus.

Jesus answered, "You are a great teacher in Israel, and you don't know this? I am telling you the truth: we speak of what we know and report what we have seen, yet none of you is willing to accept our message. You do not believe me when I tell you about the things of this world; how will you ever believe me, then, when I tell you about the things of heaven? And no one has ever gone up to heaven except the Son of Man, who came down from heaven."

As Moses lifted up the bronze snake on a pole in the desert, in the same way the Son of Man must be lifted up, so that everyone who believes in him may have eternal life. For God loved the world so much that he gave his only Son, so that everyone who believes in him may not die but have eternal life. For God did not send his Son into the world to be its judge, but to be its Savior.

*Jesus and the Woman of Samaria*

In Samaria Jesus came to a town named Sychar, which was not far from the field that Jacob had given to his son Joseph. Jacob's well was there, and Jesus, tired out by the trip, sat down by the well. It was about noon.

A Samaritan woman came to draw some water, and Jesus said to her, "Give me a drink of water." (His disciples had gone into town to buy food.)

The woman answered, "You are a Jew, and I am a Samaritan—so how can you ask me for a drink?" (Jews will not use the same cups and bowls that Samaritans use.)

Jesus answered, "If you only knew what God gives and who it is that is asking you for a drink, you would ask him, and he would give you life-giving water."

"Sir," the woman said, "you don't have a bucket and the well is deep. Where would you get that living water? It was our ancestor Jacob who gave us this well; he, his sons, and his flocks all drank from it. You don't claim to be greater than Jacob, do you?"

Jesus answered, "Whoever drinks this water will get thirsty again, but whoever drinks the water that I will give him will never be thirsty again. The water that I will give him will become in him a spring which will provide him with life-giving water and give him eternal life."

"Sir," the woman said, "give me that water! Then I will never be thirsty again, nor will I have to come here and draw water."

"Go and call your husband," Jesus told her, "and come back."

"I don't have a husband," the woman said.

Jesus replied, "You are right when you say you don't have a husband. You have been married to five men, and the man you live with now is not really your husband. You have told me the truth."

"I see you are a prophet, sir," the woman said. "My Samaritan ancestors worshiped God on this mountain, but you Jews say that Jerusalem is the place where we should worship God."

Jesus said to her, "Believe me, woman, the time will come when people will not worship the Father either on this mountain or in Jerusalem. You Samaritans do not really know whom you worship; but we Jews know whom we worship, because it is from the Jews that salvation comes. But the time is coming and is already here, when by the power of God's Spirit people will worship the Father as he really is, offering him the true worship that he wants. God is Spirit, and only by the power of his Spirit can people worship him as he really is."

The woman said to him, "I know that the Messiah will come, and when he comes, he will tell us everything."

Jesus answered, "I am he, I who am talking with you."

## Jesus Heals an Official's Son

Then Jesus went back to Cana in Galilee, where he had turned the water into wine. A government official was there whose son was sick in Capernaum. When he heard that Jesus had come from Judea to Galilee, he went to him and asked him to go to Capernaum and heal his son, who was about to die. Jesus said to him, "None of you will ever believe unless you see miracles and wonders."

"Sir" replied the official, "come with me before my child dies."

Jesus said to him, "Go, your son will live!"

The man believed Jesus' words and went. On his way home his servants met him with the news, "Your boy is going to live!"

He asked them what time it was when his son got better, and they answered, "It was one o'clock yesterday afternoon when the fever left him." Then the father remembered that it was at that very hour when Jesus had told him, "Your son will live." So he and all his family believed.

## Jesus the Bread of Life

"I am the bread of life," Jesus told them. "He who comes to me will never be hungry; he who believes in me will never be thirsty. Now, I told you that you have seen me but will not believe. Everyone whom my Father gives me will come to me. I will never turn away anyone who comes to me, because I have come down from heaven to do not my own will but the will of him who sent me. And it is the will of him who sent me that I should not lose any of all those he has given me, but that I should raise them all to life on the last day. For what my Father wants is that all who see the Son and believe in him should have eternal life: And I will raise them to life on the last day."

## Jesus Forgives a Woman in Jerusalem

Early next morning he went back to the Temple. All the people gathered round him, and he sat down and began to teach them. The teachers of the Law and the Pharisees brought in a woman who had been caught committing adultery, and they made her stand before them all. "Teacher," they said to Jesus, "this woman was caught in the very act of committing adultery. In our Law Moses commanded that such a woman must be stoned to death. Now, what do you say?" They said this to trap Jesus, so they could accuse him. But he bent over and wrote on the ground with his finger. As they stood there asking him questions, he straightened up and said to them, "Whichever one of you has committed no sin may throw the first stone at her." Then he bent over again and wrote on the ground. When they heard this, they all left, one by one, the older ones first. Jesus was left alone, with the woman still standing there. He straightened up and said to her, "Where are they? Is there no one left to condemn you?"

"No one, sir", she answered.

"Well, then," Jesus said, "I do not condemn you either. Go, but do not sin again."

### Jesus the Resurrection and the Life

One of the great signs of the power of Jesus is given in John's gospel when Jesus raises Lazarus from the dead. Jesus explains this to Martha, the sister of Lazarus.

Jesus said to her, "I am the resurrection and the life. Whoever believes in me will live, even though he dies; and whoever lives and believes in me will never die."

*Jesus the Light of the World*

Jesus spoke to the Pharisees again, "I am the light of the world," he said. "Whoever follows me will have the light of life and will never walk in darkness."

*Jesus Heals a Man Born Blind*

As Jesus was walking along, he saw a man who had been born blind. His disciples asked him, "Teacher, whose sin caused him to be born blind? Was it his own or his parents' sin?"

Jesus answered, "His blindness has nothing to do with his sins or his parents' sins. He is blind so that God's power might be seen at work in him. As long as it is day, we must do the works of him who sent me; the night is coming, when no one can work. While I am in the world, I am the light for the world."

After he said this, Jesus spat on the ground and made some mud with the spittle; he rubbed the mud on the man's eyes, and told him, "Go wash your face in the Pool of Siloam." (This name means "Sent.") So the man went, washed his face, and came back seeing.

His neighbors, then, and the people who had seen him begging before this, asked, "Isn't this the man who used to sit and beg?"

Some said, "He is the one," but others said, "No he isn't, he just looks like him."

So the man himself said, "I am the man."

"How is it that you can now see?" they asked him.

He answered, "The man called Jesus made some mud, rubbed it on my eyes, and told me to go to Siloam and wash my face! So I went, and as soon as I washed, I could see."

*The Parable of the Shepherd*

Jesus said, "I am telling you the truth: the man who does not enter the sheep pen by the gate, but climbs in some other way, is a thief and a robber. The man who goes in through the gate is the shepherd of the sheep. The gate-keeper opens the gate for him; the sheep hear his voice as he calls his own sheep by name, and he leads them out. When he has brought them out, he goes ahead of them, and the sheep follow him, because they know his voice. They will not follow someone else; instead, they will run away from such a person because they do not know his voice."

Jesus told them this parable, but they did not understand what he meant.

140

## Jesus the Good Shepherd

So Jesus said again, "I am telling you the truth: I am the gate for the sheep. All others who came before me are thieves and robbers; but the sheep did not listen to them. I am the gate. Whoever comes in by me will be saved; he will come in and go out and find pasture. The thief comes only in order to steal, kill, and destroy. I have come in order that you might have life — life in all its fullness.

"I am the good shepherd, who is willing to die for the sheep. When the hired man, who is not a shepherd and does not own the sheep, sees a wolf coming, he leaves the sheep and runs away; so the wolf snatches the sheep and scatters them. The hired man runs away because he is only a hired man and does not care about the sheep. I am the good shepherd. As the Father knows me and I know the Father, in the same way I know my sheep and they know me. And I am willing to die for them. There are other sheep which belong to me that are not in this sheep pen. I must bring them, too; they will listen to my voice, and they will become one flock with one shepherd.

"The Father loves me because I am willing to give up my life, in order that I may receive it back again. No one takes my life away from me. I give it up of my own free will. I have the right to give it up, and I have the right to take it back. This is what my Father has commanded me to do."

## Jesus Washes his Disciples' Feet

It was now the day before the Passover Festival. Jesus knew the hour had come for him to leave this world and go to the Father. He had always loved those in the world who were his own, and he loved them to the very end.

Jesus and his disciples were at supper. The Devil had already put the thought of betraying Jesus into the heart of Judas, the son of Simon Iscariot. Jesus knew that the Father had given him complete power; he knew that he had come from God and was going to God. So he rose from the table, took off his outer garment, and tied a towel round his waist. Then he poured some water into a washbasin and began to wash the disciples' feet and dry them with the towel round his waist. He came to Simon Peter, who said to him, "Are you going to wash my feet, Lord?"

Jesus answered him, "You do not understand now what I am doing, but you will understand later."

Peter declared, "Never, at any time will you wash my feet!"

"If I do not wash your feet," Jesus answered, "you will no longer be my disciple."

Simon Peter answered, "Lord, do not wash only my feet, then! Wash my hands and head, too!"

Jesus said, "Any one who has taken a bath is completely clean and does not have to wash himself, except for his feet. All of you are clean—all except one." (Jesus already knew who was going to betray him; that is why he said, "All of you, except one, are clean.")

After Jesus had washed their feet, he put his outer garment back on and returned to his place at the table. "Do you understand what I have just done to you?" he asked. "You call me Teacher and Lord, and it is right that you do so, because that is what I am. I, your Lord and Teacher, have just washed your feet. You, then, should wash one another's feet. I have set an example for you, so that you will do just what I have done for you. I tell you the truth: no slave is greater than his master, and no messenger is greater than the one who sent him. Now that you know this truth, how happy you will be if you put it into practice!"

## Jesus Speaks to his Friends at the Last Supper

*Jesus the Way to the Father*

"Do not be worried and upset," Jesus told them. "Believe in God, and believe also in me. There are many rooms in my Father's house, and I am going to prepare a place for you. I would not tell you this if it were not so. And after I go and prepare a place for you, I will come back and take you to myself, so that you will be where I am. You know the way that leads to the place where I am going."

Thomas said to him, "Lord, we do not know where you are going; how can we know the way to get there?"

Jesus answered him, "I am the way, the truth, and the life; no one goes to the Father except by me. Now that you have known me," he said to them, "you will know my Father also, and from now on you do know him, and you have seen him."

Philip said to him, "Lord, show us the Father; that is all we need."

Jesus answered, "For a long time I have been with you all; yet you do not know me, Philip? Whoever has seen me has seen the Father. Why, then, do you say, 'Show us the Father'? Do you not believe, Philip, that I am in the Father and the Father is in me? The words that I have spoken to you," Jesus said to his disciples, "do not come from me. The Father, who remains in me, does his own works. Believe me when I say that I am in the Father and the Father is in me. If not, believe because of the things I do. I am telling you the truth: whoever believes in me will do what I do — yes, he will do even greater things, because I am going to the Father. And I will do whatever you ask for in my name, so that the Father's glory will be shown through the Son. If you ask me for anything in my name, I will do it."

## The Promise of the Holy Spirit

"If you love me, you will obey my commandments. I will ask the Father, and he will give you another Helper, who will stay with you forever. He is the Spirit who reveals the truth about God. The world cannot see him or know him, because he remains with you and is in you."

"When I go, you will not be left all alone; I will come back to you. In a little while the world will see me no more, but you will see me; and because I live, you also will live. When that day comes, you will know that I am in my Father and that you are in me, just as I am in you.

"Whoever accepts my commandments and obeys them he is the one who loves me. My Father will love whoever loves me; I too will love him and reveal myself to him."

Judas (not Judas Iscariot) said, "Lord, how can it be that you will reveal yourself to us and not to the world?"

Jesus answered him, "Whoever loves me will obey my teaching. My Father will love him, and my Father and I will come to him and live with him. Whoever does not love me does not obey my teachings. And the teaching you have heard is not mine, but comes from the Father, who sent me."

"I have told you this while I am still with you. The Helper, the Holy Spirit whom the Father will send in my name, will teach you everything, and make you remember all that I have told you.

"Peace is what I leave with you; it is my own peace that I give you. I do not give it as the world does. Do not be worried and upset; do not be afraid. You heard me say to you, 'I am leaving, but I will come back to you.' If you loved me, you would be glad that I am going to the Father; for he is greater than I. I have told you this now before it all happens, so that when it does happen, you will believe. I cannot talk with you much longer, because the ruler of this world is coming. He has no power over me, but the world must know that I love the Father; that is why I do everything as he commands me."

## Jesus the Real Vine

"I am the real vine, and my Father is the gardener. He breaks off every branch in me that does not bear fruit, and prunes every branch that does bear fruit, so that it will be clean and bear more fruit. You have been made clean already by the teaching I have given to you. Remain united to me, and I will remain united to you. A branch cannot bear fruit by itself; it can do so only if it remains in the vine. In the same way you cannot bear fruit unless you remain in me."

"I am the vine, you are the branches. Whoever remains in me, and I in him, will bear much fruit; for you can do nothing without me. Whoever does not remain in me is thrown out like a branch and dries up; such branches are gathered up and thrown into the fire, where they are burned. If you remain in me and my words remain in you, then you will ask for anything you wish, and you shall have it. My Father's glory is shown by your bearing much fruit; and in this way you become my disciples. I love you just as the Father loves me; remain in my love. If you obey my commands, you will remain in my love, just as I have obeyed my Father's commands and remain in his love.

"I have told you this so that my joy may be in you and that your joy may be complete. My commandment is this: love one another, just as I love you. The greatest love a person can have for his friends is to give his life for them. And you are my friends, if you do what I command you. I do not call you servants any longer, because a servant does not know what his master is doing. Instead, I call you friends, because I have told you everything I heard from my Father. You did not choose me; I chose you and appointed you to go and bear much fruit, the kind of fruit that endures. And so the Father will give you whatever you ask of him in my name. This, then, is what I command you: love one another."

## The World's Hatred

"If the world hates you, just remember that it has hated me first. If you belonged to the world, then the world would love you as its own. But I chose you from this world, and you do not belong to it; this is why the world hates you. Remember what I told you; 'No slave is greater than his master.' If they persecuted me, they will persecute you too; if they obeyed my teaching, they will obey yours too. But they will do all this to you because you are mine; for they do not know the one who sent me. They would not have been guilty of sin if I had not come and spoken to them; as it is, they no longer have any excuse for their sin. Whoever hates me hates my Father also. They would not have been guilty of sin if I had not done among them the things that no one else ever did; as it is, they have seen what I did, and they hate both me and my Father. This must be, however, so that what is written in their Law may come true, "They hated me for no reason at all."

"The Helper will come — the Spirit who reveals the truth about God and who comes from the Father. I will send him to you from the Father, and he will speak about me. And you, too, will speak about me, because you have been with me from the very beginning."

"I have told you this so that you will not give up your faith. You will be expelled from the synagogues, and the time will come when anyone who kills you will think that by doing this he is serving God. People will do these things to you because they have not known either the Father or me. But I have told you this, so that when the time comes for them to do these things, you will remember what I told you."

## The Work of the Holy Spirit

"I did not tell you these things at the beginning, for I was with you. But now I am going to him who sent me, yet none of you asks me where I am going. And now that I have told you, your hearts are full of sadness. But I am telling you the truth: it is better for you that I go away, because if I do not go, the Helper will not come to you. But if I do go away, then I will send him to you. And when he comes, he will prove to the people of the world that they are wrong about sin and about what is right and about God's judgment. They are wrong about sin, because they do not believe in me; they are wrong about what is right, because I am going to the Father and you will not see me any more; and they are wrong about judgment, because the ruler of this world has already been judged.

"I have much more to tell you, but now it would be too much for you to bear. When however, the Spirit comes, who reveals the truth about God, he will lead you into all the truth. He will not speak on his own but he will speak of what he hears and will tell you of things to come. He will give me glory, because he will take what I say and tell it to you. All that my Father has is mine; that is why I said that the Spirit will take what I give him and tell it to you."

## Sadness and Gladness

"In a little while you will not see me any more, and then a little while later you will see me."

Some of his disciples asked among themselves, "What does this mean? He tells us that in a little while we will not see him, and then a little while later we will see him; and he also says, 'It is because I am going to the Father.' What does this 'a little while' mean? We do not know what he is talking about!"

Jesus knew that they wanted to question him, so he said to them, "I said, 'In a little while you will not see me, and then a little while later you will see me.' Is this what you are asking about among yourselves? I am telling the truth: you will cry and weep, but the world will be glad; you will be sad, but your sadness will turn into gladness. When a woman is about to give birth, she is sad because her hour of suffering has come; but when the baby is born, she forgets her suffering, because she is happy that a baby has been born into the world. That is how it is with you: now you are sad, but I will see you again, and your hearts will be filled with gladness, the kind of gladness that no one can take away from you.

"When that day comes, you will not ask me for anything. I am telling you the truth: the Father will give you whatever you ask of him in my name. Until now you have not asked for anything in my name; ask and you will receive, so that your happiness may be complete."

146

*Victory over the World*

"I have used figures of speech to tell you these things. But the time will come when I will not use figures of speech, but will speak to you plainly about the Father. When that day comes, you will ask him in my name; and I do not say that I will ask him on your behalf, for the Father himself loves you. He loves you because you love me and have believed that I came from God. I did come from the Father, and I came into the world; and now I am leaving the world and going to the Father."

Then his disciples said to him, "Now, you are speaking plainly without using figures of speech. We know now that you know everything; you do not need to have someone to ask you questions. This makes us believe that you came from God."

Jesus answered them, "Do you believe now? The time is coming, and is already here, when all of you will be scattered, each one to his own home, and I will be left all alone. But I am not really alone, because the Father is with me. I have told you this so that you will have peace by being united to me. The world will make you suffer. But be brave! I have defeated the world!"

*Jesus Prays for his Friends before his Death*

After Jesus finished saying this, he looked up to heaven and said, "Father, the hour has come. Give glory to your Son, so that the Son may give glory to you. For you gave him authority over all mankind, so that he might give eternal life to all those you gave him. And eternal life means to know you, the only true God, and to know Jesus Christ, whom you sent. I have shown your glory on earth; I have finished the work you gave me to do. Father! Give me glory in your presence now, the same glory I had with you before the world was made.

"I have made you known to those you gave me out of the world. They belonged to you, and you gave them to me. They have obeyed your word, and now they know that everything you gave me comes from you. I gave them the message that you gave me, and they received it; they know that it is true that I came from you, and they believe that you sent me.

"I pray for them. I do not pray for the world but for those you gave me, for they belong to you. All I have is yours, and all you have is mine; and my glory is shown through them. And now I am coming to you; I am no longer in the world, but they are in the world. Holy Father! Keep them safe by the power of your name, the name you gave me, so that they may be one just as you and I are one. While I was with them I kept them safe by the power of your name, the name you gave me. I protected them, and not one of them was lost, except the man who was bound to be lost — so that the scripture might come true. And now I am coming to you, and I say these things in the world so that they might have my joy in their hearts, in all its fullness. I gave them your message, and the world hated them, because they do not belong to the world, just as I do not belong to the world. I do not ask you to take them out of the world, but I do ask you to keep them safe from the Evil One. Just as I do not belong to the world, they do not belong to the world. Dedicate them to yourself by means of the truth; your word is truth. I sent them into the world, just as you sent me into the world. And for their sake I dedicate myself to you, in order that they, too, may be truly dedicated to you.

"I pray not only for them, but also for those who believe in me because of their message. I pray that they may all be one. Father! May they be in us, just as you are in me and I am in you. May they be one, so that the world will believe that you sent me. I gave them the same glory you gave me, so that they may be one, just as you and I are one: I in them and you in me, so that they may be completely one, in order that the world may know that you sent me and that you love them as you love me.

"Father! You have given them to me, and I want them to be with me where I am, so that they may see my glory, the glory you gave me, for you loved me before the world was made. Righteous Father! The world does not know you, but I know you, and these know that you sent me. I made you known to them, and I will continue to do so, in order that the love you have for me may be in them, and so that I also may be in them."

## Conclusion

Now, there are many other things that Jesus did. If they were all written down one by one, I suppose that the whole world could not hold the books that would be written.

# 9
# How to Follow Jesus

*Luke wrote a second book after his gospel: The Acts of the Apostles. He told how Christianity spread from Jerusalem to Rome because it was filled with the power of God, the Holy Spirit.*

*Some letters of John have survived, and they show the love and the hope which gave such joy to Christian life.*

*Some of Paul's letters were also treasured, and they help us to understand that his love and hope can still produce great joy, whenever anyone learns from Jesus what love means.*

## Why the Apostles Acted

*Luke writes*

*Jesus Is Taken up to Heaven*

When the apostles met together with Jesus they asked him, "Lord, will you at this time give the Kingdom back to Israel?"

Jesus said to them, "The times and occasions are set by my Father's own authority, and it is not for you to know when they will be. But when the Holy Spirit comes on you, you will be filled with power, and you will be witnesses for me in Jerusalem, in all of Judea and Samaria, and to the ends of the earth." After saying this, he was taken up to heaven as they watched him; and a cloud hid them from their sight.

They still had their eyes fixed on the sky as he went away, when two men dressed in white suddenly stood beside them, and said, "Galileans, why are you standing there looking up at the sky? This Jesus, who was taken from you into heaven, will come back in the same way that you saw him go to heaven."

Then the apostles went back to Jerusalem from the Mount of Olives, which is about half a mile away from the city. They entered the city and went up to the room where they were staying: Peter, John, James and Andrew, Philip and Thomas, Bartholomew and Matthew, James, the son of Alphaeus, Simon the Patriot, and Judas the son of James. They gathered frequently to pray as a group, together with the women and with Mary the mother of Jesus, and with his brothers.

## The Coming of the Holy Spirit

When the day of Pentecost came, all the believers were gathered together in one place. Suddenly there was a noise from the sky which sounded like a strong wind blowing, and it filled the whole house where they were sitting. Then they saw what looked like tongues of fire which spread out and touched each person there. They were all filled with the Holy Spirit and began to talk in other languages, as the Spirit enabled them to speak.

There were Jews living in Jerusalem, religious men who had come from every country in the world. When they heard this noise, a large crowd gathered. They were all excited, because each one of them heard the believers talking in his own language. In amazement and wonder they exclaimed, "These people who are talking like this are Galileans! How is it, then, that all of us hear them speaking in our own native language? We are from Parthia, Media, and Elam; from Mesopotamia, Judea, and Cappadocia; from Pontus and Asia, from Phrygia and Pamphylia, from Egypt and the regions of Libya near Cyrene. Some of us are from Rome, both Jews and Gentiles converted to Judaism, and some of us are from Crete and Arabia — yet all of us hear them speaking in our own languages about the great things that God has done!" Amazed and confused, they all kept asking each other, "What does this mean?"

But others made fun of the believers, saying, "These people are drunk!"

## Peter's Message

Then Peter stood up with the other eleven apostles, and in a loud voice began to speak to the crowd, "Fellow Jews and all of you who live in Jerusalem, listen to me and let me tell you what this means. These people are not drunk, as you suppose; it is only nine o'clock in the morning. Instead, this what the prophet Joel spoke about.

'This is what I will do in the last days, God says:
    I will pour out my Spirit on everyone.
Your sons and your daughters will proclaim my message;
        your young men will see visions,
        and your old men will dream dreams.' "

Peter made his appeal to them and with many other words he urged them, saying, "Save yourselves from the punishment coming on this wicked people!" Many of them believed his message, and were baptized, about three thousand people were added to the group that day. They spent their time in learning from the apostles, taking part in the fellowship, and sharing in the fellowship meals and the prayers.

*Life among the Believers*

Many miracles and wonders were done through the apostles, and everyone was filled with awe. All the believers continued together in close fellowship and shared their belongings with one another. They would sell their property and possessions, and distribute the money among all, according to what each one needed. Day after day they met as a group in the Temple, and they had their meals together in their homes, eating with glad and humble hearts, praising God and enjoying the good will of all the people. And every day the Lord added to their group those who were being saved.

## John Writes about God's Love

*Children of God*

See how much the Father has loved us! His love is so great that we are called God's children — and so, in fact, we are. This is why the world does not know us: it has not known God. My dear friends, we are now God's children, but it is not yet clear what we shall become. But we know that when Christ appears, we shall become like him, because we shall see him as he really is. Everyone who has this hope in Christ keeps himself pure, just as Christ is pure.

Whoever sins is guilty of breaking God's law because sin is a breaking of the law. You know that Christ appeared in order to take away sins, and that there is no sin in him. So everyone who lives in union with Christ does not continue to sin; but whoever continues to sin has never seen him or known him.

Let no one deceive you, my children! Whoever does what is right is righteous, just as Christ is righteous. Whoever continues to sin belongs to the Devil, because the Devil has sinned from the very beginning. The Son of God appeared for this very reason, to destroy what the Devil had done.

Whoever is a child of God does not continue to sin, for God's very nature is in him; and because God is his Father, he cannot continue to sin. Here is the clear difference between God's children and the Devil's children: anyone who does not do what is right or does not love his brother is not God's child.

*God Is Love*

Dear friends, let us love one another, because love comes from God. Whoever loves is a child of God and knows God. Whoever does not love does not know God, because God is love. And God showed his love

152

for us by sending his only Son into the world, so that we might have life through him. This is what love is: it is not that we have loved God, but that he loved us and sent his Son to be the means by which our sins are forgiven.

Dear friends, if this is how God loved us, then we should love one another. No one has ever seen God, but if we love one another, God lives in union with us, and his love is made perfect in us.

We are sure that we live in union with God and he lives in union with us, because he has given us his Spirit. And we have seen and tell others that the Father sent his Son to be the Savior of the world. If anyone declares that Jesus is the Son of God, he lives in union with God and God lives in union with him. And we ourselves know and believe the love which God has for us.

God is love, and whoever lives in love lives in union with God and God lives in union with him. Love is made perfect in us in order that we may have courage on the Judgment Day; and we will have it because our life in this world is the same as Christ's. There is no fear in love; perfect love drives out all fear. So then, love has not been made perfect in anyone who is afraid, because fear has to do with punishment.

We love because God first loved us. If someone says, he loves but hates his brother, he is a liar. For he cannot love God, whom he has not seen, if he does not love his brother, whom he has seen. The command that Christ has given us is this: whoever loves God must love his brother also.

## A Prayer in the Letter to the Ephesians

For this reason I fall on my knees before the Father, from whom every family in heaven and on earth receives its true name. I ask God from the wealth of his glory to give you power through his Spirit to be strong in your inner selves, and I pray that Christ will make his home in your hearts through faith. I pray that you may have your roots and foundations in love, so that you, together with all God's people, may have the power to understand how broad and long, how high and deep, is Christ's love. Yes, may you come to know his love — although it can never be fully known — and so be completely filled with the very nature of God.

To him who by means of his power working in us is able to do so much more than we can ever ask for, or even think of: to God be the glory in the church and in Christ Jesus, for all time, forever and ever! Amen.

## Unity and Love: Paul Writes to the Corinthians

*One Body with Many Parts*

Christ is like a single body, which has many parts; it is still one body, even though it is made up of different parts. In the same way, all of us, whether Jews or Gentiles, whether slaves or free, men, have been baptized into the one body by the same Spirit, and we have all been given the one Spirit to drink.

For the body itself is not made up of only one part, but of many parts. If the foot were to say, "Because I am not a hand, I don't belong to the body," that would not keep it from being a part of the body. And if the ear were to say, "Because I am not an eye, I don't belong to the body," that would not keep it from being a part of the body. If the whole body were just an eye, how could it hear? And if it were only an ear, how could it smell? As it is, however, God put every different part in the body just as he wanted it to be. There would not be a body if it were all only one part! As it is, there are many parts and one body.

So then, the eye cannot say to the hand, "I don't need you!" Nor can the head say to the feet, "Well, I don't need you!" On the contrary, we cannot do without the parts of the body that seem to be weaker; and those parts that we think aren't worth very much are the ones which we treat with greater care; while the parts of the body which don't look very nice are treated with special modesty, which the more beautiful parts do not need. God himself has put the body together in such a way as to give greater honor to those parts that need it. And so there is no division in the body, but all its different parts have the same concern for one another. If one part of the body suffers, all the other parts suffer with it; if one part is praised, all the other parts share its happiness.

All of you are Christ's body, and each one is a part of it. In the church God has put all in place: in the first place apostles, in the second place prophets, and in the third place teachers; then those who perform miracles, followed by those who are given the power to heal or to help others or to direct them or to speak in strange tongues. They are not all apostles or prophets or teachers. Not everyone has power to work miracles or to heal diseases or to speak in strange tongues or to explain what is said. Set your hearts, then, on the more important gifts.

Best of all, however, is the following way.

*Love*

I may be able to speak the languages of men and even of angels, but if I have no love, my speech is no more than a noisy gong or a clanging bell. I may have the gift of inspired preaching; I may have all knowledge and understand all secrets; I may have all the faith needed to move mountains

— but if I have no love, I am nothing. I may give away everything I have, and even give up my body to be burned — but if I have no love, this does me no good.

Love is patient and kind; it is not jealous or conceited or proud; love is not ill-mannered or selfish or irritable; love does not keep a record of wrongs; love is not happy with evil, but is happy with the truth. Love never gives up: and its faith, hope, and patience never fail.

Love is eternal. These are inspired messages, but they are temporary; there are gifts of speaking in strange tongues, but they will cease; there is knowledge, but it will pass. For our gifts of knowledge and of inspired messages are only partial; but when what is perfect comes, then what is partial will disappear.

When I was a child, my speech, feelings, and thinking were all those of a child; now that I am a man, I have no more use for childish ways. What we see now is like a dim image in a mirror; then we shall see face to face. What I know now is only partial; then it will be complete — as complete as God's knowledge of me.

Meanwhile these three remain: faith, hope, and love; and the greatest of these is love.

### Paul's Prayer

The grace of the Lord Jesus Christ, the love of God, and the fellowship of the Holy Spirit be with you all.

## The Christian Life in Paul's Letters

### Father, my Father!

To show that you are his sons, God sent the Spirit of his Son into our hearts, the Spirit who cries out, "Father, my Father." So then, you are no longer a slave but a son. And since you are his son, God will give you all that he has for his sons.

### The Spirit and Human Nature

What I say is this: let the Spirit direct your lives, and you will not satisfy the desires of the human nature. For what our human nature wants is opposed to what the Spirit wants, and what the Spirit wants is opposed to what human nature wants. These two are enemies, and this means that you cannot do what you want to do. If the Spirit leads you, then you are not subject to the Law.

What human nature does is quite plain. It shows itself in immoral, filthy, and indecent actions; in worship of idols and witchcraft. People become enemies and they fight; they become jealous, angry, and ambitious. They separate into parties and groups; they are envious, get drunk, have orgies, and do other things like these. I warn you now as I have before: those who do these things will not possess the Kingdom of God.

But the Spirit produces love, joy, peace, patience, kindness, goodness, faithfulness, humility, and self-control. There is no law against such things as these. And those who belong to Christ Jesus have put to death their human nature with all its passions and desires. The Spirit has given us life; he must also control our lives. We must not be proud or irritate one another or be jealous of one another.

### The Power of the Gospel

I have complete confidence in the gospel; it is God's power to save all who believe, first the Jews and also the Gentiles. For the gospel reveals how God puts people right with himself: it is through faith from beginning to end. As the scripture says, "The person who is put right with God through faith shall live."

### The Whole Armor of God

Build up your strength in union with the Lord and by means of his mighty power. Put on all the armor that God gives you, so that you will be able to stand up against the Devil's evil tricks. For we are not fighting against human beings but against the wicked spiritual forces in the heavenly world, the rulers, authorities, and cosmic powers of this dark age. So put on God's armor now! Then when the evil day comes, you will be able to resist the enemy's attacks, and after fighting to the end, you will still hold your ground.

So stand ready; with truth as a belt tight round your waist, with righteousness as your breastplate, and as your shoes the readiness to announce the Good News of peace. At all times carry faith as a shield; for with it you will be able to put out all the burning arrows shot by the Evil One. And accept salvation as a helmet, and the word of God as the sword which the Spirit gives you. Do all this in prayer, asking for God's help. Pray on every occasion, as the Spirit leads. For this reason keep alert and never give up; pray always for all God's people. And pray also for me, that God will give me a message when I am ready to speak, so that I may speak boldly and make known the gospel's secret. For the sake of this gospel I am an ambassador, though now I am in prison. Pray that I may be bold in speaking about the gospel as I should.

I want you to know, my brothers, that the things that have happened to me have really helped the progress of the gospel. As a result, the whole palace guard and all the others here know that I am in prison because I am a servant of Christ. And my being in prison has given most of the brothers more confidence in the Lord, so that they grow bolder all the time to preach the message fearlessly.

Of course some of them preach Christ because they are jealous and quarrelsome, but others from genuine good will. These do so from love, because they know that God has given me the work of defending the gospel. The others do not proclaim Christ sincerely, but from a spirit of selfish ambition; they think that they will make more trouble for me while I am in prison.

It does not matter! I am happy about it — just so Christ is preached in every way possible, whether from wrong or right motives. And I will continue to be happy, because I know that by means of your prayers and the help which comes from the Spirit of Jesus Christ I shall be set free. My deep desire and hope is that I shall never fail in my duty, but that at all times, and especially right now, I shall be full of courage, so that with my whole being I shall bring honor to Christ, whether I live or die. For what is life? To me, it is Christ. Death, then, will bring more. But if by continuing to live I can do more worthwhile work, then I am not sure which I should choose. I am pulled in two directions. I want very much to leave this life and be with Christ, which is a far better thing; but for your sake it is much more important that I remain alive. I am sure of this, and so I know that I will stay. I will stay on with you all, to add to your progress and joy in the faith, so that when I am with you again you will have even more reason to be proud of me in your life in union with Christ Jesus.

Now, the important thing is that your way of life should be as the gospel of Christ requires, so that, whether or not I am able to go and see you, I will hear that you are standing firm with one common purpose and that with only one desire you are fighting together for the faith of of the gospel. Don't be afraid of your enemies; always be courageous, and this will prove to them that they will lose and that you will win, because it is God who gives you the victory. For you have been given the privilege of serving Christ, not only by believing in him, but also by suffering for him. Now you can take part with me in the battle. It is the same battle you saw me fighting in the past, and as you hear the one I am fighting still.

## Christian Joy and Peace

May you always be joyful in your union with the Lord. I say it again: rejoice!

Show a gentle attitude toward everyone. The Lord is coming soon. Don't worry about anything, but in all your prayers ask God for what you need, always asking him with a thankful heart. And God's peace, which is far beyond human understanding, will keep your hearts and minds safe in union with Christ Jesus.

In conclusion, my brothers, fill your minds with those things that are good and that deserve praise: things that are true, noble, right, pure, lovely, and honorable. Put into practice what you learned and received from me, both from my words and from my actions. And the God who gives us peace will be with you.

## Running toward the Goal

I do not claim that I have already succeeded or have already become perfect. I keep striving to win the prize for which Christ Jesus has already won me to himself. Of course my brothers, I really do not think that I have already won it; the one thing I do, however, is to forget what is behind me and do my best to reach what is ahead. So I run straight toward the goal in order to win the prize, which is God's call through Christ Jesus to the life above.

## Paul's Farewell

As for me, the hour has come for me to be sacrificed; the time is here for me to leave this life. I have done my best in the race, I have run the full distance and I have kept the faith. And now there is waiting for me the prize of victory awarded for a righteous life, the prize which the Lord, the righteous Judge, will give me on that Day — and not only to me, but to all those who wait with love for him to appear.